PROFESSIONAL WORK AND MARRIAGE

An East–West Comparison

PROFESSIONAL WORK AND MARRIAGE

An East–West Comparison

Marilyn Rueschemeyer

St. Martin's Press   New York

Library of Congress Cataloging in Publication Data

Rueschemeyer, Marilyn, 1938–
   Professional work and marriage.

   Bibliography: p.
   Includes index.
1. Professions—United States—Case studies.
2. Professions—Europe, Eastern—Case studies.
3. Women in the professions—United States—Case
studies. 4. Women in the professions—Europe,
Eastern—Case studies. 5. Married people—Employment—United States—Case studies. 6. Married
people—Employment—Europe, Eastern—Case studies.
I. Title.
HT687.R83   1981   306.8′7   80–39959
ISBN 0-312-64782-4

For Julia and Simone, with love and hope

Contents

Acknowledgements

I would like to express my gratitude to Gordon Fellman, Kristine Rosenthal, Charlotte Weissberg and George Ross for their advice and strong encouragement throughout this research. I also thank Kurt Wolff, who wrote on my behalf to a friend in the German Democratic Republic, and Janet Giele, Peter Evans, Josef Gugler, Ann Seidman and Richard Quinney, who made very helpful comments on the manuscript. Archie Brown's suggestions for the Eastern European sections of the manuscript were of great value; for his kindness as well as the warm hospitality of all my colleagues at St Antony's College, Oxford, I am indeed grateful.

My husband, Dietrich Rueschemeyer, shared my excitement, ideas and worries about this project from its beginning and continued to be involved and encouraging despite his own professional commitments. Without his support and without the patience and practical help of our daughters, Julia and Simone, I would have never completed this project.

Finally, during this research I met men and women who not only answered my questions but tried to share a part of their lives, their ideas, their dreams of a good society with me. I will never forget them.

Providence, Rhode Island   MARILYN RUESCHEMEYER

1 The problem stated: Ambitions and work pressures, their origins and consequences in Capitalist and Socialist Societies

Strains within the family, tensions and problems between husbands and wives as well as between parents and children are a recurrent theme in private conversations, journals of opinion and the lecture circuit. There is a sense that the roles of men and women are undergoing a profound change and that life in the family is becoming increasingly difficult. Yet our understanding of these issues is very limited. Many realize that the individualistic formula of common wisdom, 'it all depends on the people involved', is not sufficient. However, public debates which go beyond such simplistic commentary often focus narrowly on the family as it is presently structured. The question then becomes: what precisely is wrong with the contemporary family? The more conservative answers urge a return to and a revitalization of the inherited forms of marriage and family life. Thus, the 'Total Woman' (Morgan, 1976) is to recreate a loving family and a romantic marriage by submitting herself to the needs of her husband, by organizing her work at home so that it does not overwhelm her and by trying to introduce variety and surprise into her personal and erotic style in order to keep her husband's interest when he returns from work.

Increasing numbers, especially of educated women, are sympathetic to the feminist argument that it is the very role of the woman in the family as it is presently structured that is at the heart of her difficulties, and ultimately of the difficulties of her husband and children as well. The woman – and her family – would be far better off if she were able to turn some of her energies and interests elsewhere, in particular to the work place where she could directly

1

participate in the wider society and gain recognition and self-respect. She would be happier and her family life, if she chooses to have one, would be healthier.

In this book I explore one important aspect of personal life in marriage and the family – how it is affected by pressures and ambitions to perform at work. Personal life in marriage, family and friendship relations cannot be understood in isolation from other involvements and the institutional structures that shape them. Work is for most people the major involvement outside the private sphere, and the work of women outside the family is central to the debate between opposing visions of a satisfactory marriage and family life. This study compares the personal and professional life of men and women in the United States with similar experiences in two socialist societies, the Soviet Union and the German Democratic Republic.

The nature of professional work makes it particularly suitable for an investigation of the impact of work pressures and ambitions on personal life outside work. Based on prolonged academic study, professional work tends to become a 'central life interest' of its practitioners (Dubin, 1956; Orzack, 1959). It is often intrinsically meaningful and personally fulfilling. Furthermore, it is a strong basis for respect from others, self-regard and dignity. Both in capitalist and socialist societies, professionals have some role in defining the problems they work on; they take part in determining how the work will be done and in creating their time schedules, they often participate in decisions concerning the result of their work, and they identify with the professional community – or at least some part of their profession with its shared competence, language and spirit.

That the nature of work is crucial for the quality of people's lives has long been recognized. Marx wrote about the 'alienation' of workers in capitalist society, the dissociation of labour from the worker's material and immaterial interests and from his personal life. Building on Marx's analysis, Blauner has investigated how lack of autonomy and power in the work place, meaningless work, social isolation and self-estrangement are in varying degree experienced by manual workers in contemporary America (Marx, 1844/1963; Blauner, 1964). In comparison with blue-collar and routine white-collar work, professionals clearly suffer least from these different forms of alienation. This suggests that professional work provides ideal conditions for a fulfilled and harmonious life. However, such a conclusion may be premature. The very fact that professional work tends to be of fundamental personal importance often turns work into an all-embracing concern. Total absorption in one's work and the assumption of pervasive responsibilities at work may leave little room for other concerns. In particular, such work commitment may severely impair one's personal life with 'significant others' outside work. The fact that the work of professionals is relatively free from alienation and that it is at the same time – and for largely the same reasons – potentially destructive of a meaningful personal life outside work might be called the 'paradox of professional work' in contemporary society. What this book explores, then, are the conditions which shape the balance between work involvement and personal life outside work among professionals.

The problems of combining strong work involvement with rich and fulfilling personal relations in family and friendships have been familiar for a long time to many men and women in the United States and in other countries. Yet social theory and research have tended to neglect a realistic analysis of the connections, and in particular the tensions, between these two spheres of life. In the typical analysis, the husband and father's work involvement represents the major tie of family to the larger society. His income and the prestige of his position determine the status of the family. Where tensions and pressures at work are recognized, coming home from work has generally been seen as a return to an 'innocent and whole' world, to an area of recovery for the husband from the harsh outside, to a place where he can be honest, emotional and loving. Family life thus is governed by other rules, other expectations of behaviour; it is a separate world. Where the interrelations between home and work have been investigated they have typically been viewed as harmonious and well integrated (Kanter, 1977).

Studies of dual-career couples come closest to what is at issue here (see Rapoport and Rapoport, 1971; Holmstrom, 1972; Rapoport and Rapoport, 1976) and they did advance our knowledge of the problems and policy issues raised by the increasing numbers of women who engage in full-time work outside the house, while their husbands are active in work, too. They focused primarily on how dual careers can be accommodated in people's lives. My work broadens and shifts the emphasis of inquiry, relating differences in the attitudes toward one's career to social relations in the place of work and to the wider institutional structure that shapes ambitions and social relations in professional work. At the same time, it asks how these different conditions affect personal relations in family and friendship.

The tensions between work and family life and the fragmentation of individual existence that often derive from their separation into different social spheres, then, are the central concern of this study. Since investigations of these problems are relatively sparse, my goal was to generate ideas and insights about the impact of work pressures – shaped by different institutions in different countries – on personal life in marriage, family and friendship rather than to test systematically pre-formulated hypotheses in an inclusive survey study. Thus, I decided to conduct several series of intensive interviews and to explore these problems in depth through the thoughts, feelings and interpretations of the men and women I spoke with. Altogether, I did seventy-three such interviews, supplemented later by a dozen more interviews on closely related topics.

Even though a person's current life situation is crucial for shaping attitudes toward work, success and competitiveness as well as personal relations in family and friendship, these attitudes do have their roots in earlier experiences, particularly in family and school. While memories going back into one's childhood and adolescence do not constitute very reliable evidence, they can give important clues for the interpretation of later patterns of living. In my talks, I therefore focused first on the present situation of the men and women I spoke with and then explored the past from there. I looked at the present situation at work, the different stages of the professional's career in order to determine periods of particular stress or satisfaction, initial career choices and the development of ambitions. Considerations of the past included parents' occupational status, experiences in childhood and finally the aspirations and pressures to achieve and conform in school.

Ideally, I might have interviewed both husband and wife in each family. Yet I initially decided against this because it seemed a powerful interference in the marital relationship, which I preferred to avoid; it also did not appear to be necessary for my purposes to have an opportunity to confront the two versions with each other. In my talks with Soviet and East German professionals, however, I did not always have a choice because of the difficulties of finding interview partners. I therefore spoke with five married couples. These interviews evoked in me a curiosity to speak with both partners in some of the American families as well. Would there be differences in their perceptions and interpretations and in their approach to their marriage and work lives? I decided to include three couples among my American respondents, too.

My analysis is structured by two comparisons. The first is the comparison of the impact of work on families where only the husband practises a profession (single-career families) with the effects of work involvement on families where both husband and wife are active in professional work (dual-career families). A major guiding idea of this study was that the marital relationship would be very differently affected by work pressures if the wife also worked professionally outside the house than if she stayed at home. This comparison is explored primarily in my American interviews because single-career families are rare among professionals in the socialist societies of Eastern Europe. I interviewed forty American men and women in the Providence–Boston area.[1] Roughly half of these respondents were employed in the public and non-profit sectors and half worked in private business corporations.

The second basic comparison contrasts work and family patterns of professionals in the United States with those in two socialist countries, the Soviet Union and the German Democratic Republic. This gives us the opportunity to explore more broadly how pressures at work and the role professional ambitions play in individual lives are influenced by the wider institutional structure of a society, by the contrasts between socialism and capitalism in political culture as well as in economic and social structure. By looking at the links between professional work and personal life in these different social contexts, we not only go beyond the common focus on individual personality differences – how tense or relaxed, aggressive or more easily contented, resourceful or inefficient a given person happens to be – but also avoid taking the dominant features of our own culture and socio-economic institutions for granted. I therefore decided to explore the same questions with professionals from the Soviet Union and the German Democratic Republic and to compare them with the picture yielded by my American interviews.

I spoke first with thirty-three professional men and women who lived in the Soviet Union and the German Democratic Republic. These talks were supplemented three years later with a dozen more interviews in the German Democratic Republic. Although my interest was then on the work collective of academic women, several of the questions covered the central themes investigated here. These interviews supported my major findings. The focus of all of these interviews was not on the ideal patterns of life in socialism as envisioned by socialist theorists and anti-socialist critics but on the concrete experiences in family and work in these two countries as seen by the men and women I spoke with.[2]

Professional work and the development of ambition in the United States

Work in industrial society, taken out of the home, puts pressure on the individual to fulfil the demands of a particular institution, to live up to its expectations and to behave accordingly, even outside work.[3] Yet it would be a mistake to think of professional men and women as simply being 'ruled over' by professional or managerial elites. As I suggested before, professionals have a greater degree of autonomy at work than most other workers. Furthermore, through socialization – the actual process of becoming a member of the profession – most individuals come to identify with their work roles, to feel them as an integral part of their being.[4] Professional education and early practice are experiences crucial for the development of ambition and commitment. The practices and attitudes prevailing during this time when the personal identification with the profession forms, have a long-lasting effect on the lives of most practitioners.

Nearly all the professionals I spoke to wanted to be good at what they were doing. All of them measured the goals of being successful, of achieving, by very high standards. Their success in meeting these aspirations led to a sense of accomplishment and satisfaction, but it also appeared that these high standards and feelings of having to work hard in order to 'make it' or simply to be 'worthy' were also a cause of strain for many of them.

Very much related to and persistently complicating the problem of having to work hard in order to 'make it' is the question of what 'making it' really means and whether there is ever a point where most people sit back with feelings of relief, with a sense of adequate accomplishment. In my talks, I tried to identify those phases in a career that were particularly filled with tension. I explored how limitations of ambition and stable satisfaction came about, if at all, and what the consequences for family relations were in the long run of the way in which high-tension phases were handled.

A professional's values and personal expectations are not independent of the demands of colleagues, clients and the institutions he or she works for. Norms and standards are constantly inculcated and maintained by pressures and rewards. These influences shape personal aspirations. Expressions of commitment to high standards are taken as equally important as specific performances. Especially among professionals, there is clearly a social control of personal commitment.[5] It is precisely because of the inner acceptance of these work norms that it becomes difficult to separate them from external work pressures; if they are fully internalized, they may not be experienced any more as pressures from the outside but as one's own goals and aspirations.

The work settings of my respondents varied greatly. They included individual practitioners as well as employees of professional organizations such as law firms, hospitals, and symphony orchestras. What were the differences they perceived in their careers, in their independence, in the possibilities for self-scheduling and in pressures to perform? What were the effects of being self-employed or employed by a bureaucracy, in a private business corporation or in a non-profit organization? The differences must not be simplistically overstated. For instance, even in bureaucracies, entrepreneurial qualities are often required and success may depend on selling services or products to a client interested in buying them (Vollmer and Mills, 1966, p. 276). In certain organizations there is built-in conflict, such as competition for scarce resources within the organization itself (Kahn et al., 1964, p. 90). Professionals may have tensions working in bureaucracies and resist bureaucratic rules and bureaucratic supervision (Scott, 1966, p. 269).

Although the pressures described in the interviews vary to a degree, professionals as well as businessmen are all in situations which place great demands on their time and which involve much responsibility, however specialized the domain. Wilenski (1963) found that while other workers enjoy increased leisure, the working hours of professionals, as well as executives, officials and the self-employed have remained high. Hospitals, law firms, universities and business firms are organized with institutional goals in mind. The work organization's demands are often at odds with other expectations an individual may face and with his own personal concerns.[6] These frictions and discrepancies often become in effect a message to the individual to look out for himself as the institution looks after its own interests. However, this option is limited for professionals, if not completely closed, by the various ways in which personal work commitments, aspirations and anxieties are harnessed to the organizational purpose. The tensions that arise at work as well as the fact that the demands of work are less than well tailored to the needs of daily life have consequences for personal relations outside work. To these we turn now.

The effects of work pressures and ambitions on personal life in the United States

A number of studies of the effects of pressures and ambitions on human relationships have focused on executives, managers and high-level businessmen. The personality of the executive is said to be composite of many of the attitudes and values accepted by middle-class Americans.

Acquisitiveness and achievement, self-directedness and independent thought, are in this group counter-balanced by uncertainty, constant activity, the continual fear of losing ground and the inability to be introspectively casual (Warner and Martin, 1959, p. 24).

Whyte (1956, pp. 287–404) discussed the limited nature of friendships that develop among career-minded organization men. Warner and Abegglen (1963) noted their single-minded devotion to work. In *Men and Masculinity* (edited by Pleck and Sawyer), Fernando Bartolmé (1974) included an executive's view on developing the independence of his children:

Doing things is more important than people . . . I want my children to learn to ski well. In skiing, one needs man and hill; nobody else is needed (p. 102).

The executives Bartolmé met felt drained and unable to communicate very much with their families when they returned home. Emmanuel Kay (1974), in his discussion of the working conditions of middle management, inequitable salaries, job insecurity and lack of authority over policies, related these to the development of low self-esteem,[7] alcoholism, marital problems and obsolescence on the job. Bailyn (1977) found important relations between the professional self-esteem of men in management and technological work and their accommodation to the demands of family life. The men who are responsive to these demands, have 'overall less self-confidence and show less interest in the intrinsic character of the work they do' (p. 126). 'Almost none of the respondents with high involvement are accommodative to their families' (p. 128).

Many analyses of these problems tend to be general characterizations of the culture. Karen Horney (1937) was very concerned about the relationship between pressures and ambitions at work, generally, and personal relations; her main interest was the effect on the personality, the lack of self-worth that an ideology of self-determining success creates. Erich Fromm (1962) feared the development of human beings who are completely adapted to the demands of the market place, people who see themselves and others as commodities. Ashley Montagu (1962) wrote that to talk about love and competition in the same breath was impossible:

No amount of semantic jugglery can reconcile competition and love. If you are socialized in a competitive society, you will become insecure, fearful, anxious and unloving (p. 55).

Seeley et al. (1956, pp. 229–30) were concerned about the development of covert competition even in children; others discussed the development of a suburban life style and loss of community (Seeley et al., 1956; Stein, 1960).

These authors present us with general cultural interpretations of the source of occupational tensions and its effects; at the end of my study, I will return to these broader ideas, including alienation, and interpret my findings against this background.

Initially, however, I concentrate on the details of what is actually happening to people in their personal lives.

I did not project my picture of the way families and friends should be together; rather, I sought to elicit from the people I interviewed their ideal preferences of what marital and friendship relations should be like as well as the priorities expressed in behaviour. I have asked concrete questions about the daily lives of my respondents in order to determine if and how pressures related to work influence human relations; whether there are time limitations, feelings of exhaustion, absent-mindedness at home and an inability to 'tune-in' with personal, non-instrumental relations, feelings of frustration and perhaps displaced aggression. I tried to identify different inadequacies in personal interaction as perceived by my respondents and to relate them to different work experiences and to the career patterns and socialization experiences that stood behind the present work situation.

A serious problem in interpersonal matters can be handled in various ways. At one extreme, it can touch off a vicious cycle of action and reaction that leads to increasing estrangement from each other. At the other extreme, an occasional interference with a satisfying relation may simply be shrugged off; it may pass without long-range consequences. I wondered if variations in how interferences derived from work were absorbed related to other characteristics of my respondents. Would it make a difference if a couple had a traditional marriage in a traditional setting, with firm and widely shared expectations of feminine and masculine role behaviour? What was the effect of the Women's Movement on a traditional marriage? To such questions, I shall plainly not be able to give definitive answers since my sample is small. However, since my interviews are varied and rich in detail, I feel able to develop important insights and plausible hypotheses about these matters.

The comparison with Eastern European socialist societies

For the interpretation of my interviews with professionals from socialist countries a discussion of certain basic features of these societies is necessary. The Soviet Union and the German Democratic Republic are in certain ways similar to the United

States. While they differ in cultural heritage, all three countries are modern societies with highly industrialized sectors. Yet the two socialist countries have a lower standard of living, in part because they are less developed economically, in part because of the devastations of the Second World War. The changes that occurred with socialism in Eastern Europe were not only ideological but structural as well. The different role of profit maximization based on different forms of ownership of the means of production, differences in job security and other social supports, and possibly contrasts in competitiveness at work seem potentially very important for my interests.

Changes in the roles of women in socialist societies allow me to explore further the effects of participation of women in the labour force. Work outside the household has become a firmly established norm for women in the Soviet Union and the German Democratic Republic, while the return of middle-class American women in large numbers to the labour force is a relatively recent phenomenon.[8] In the United States it is an individual option, chosen with increasing frequency, while in the socialist countries of Eastern Europe, because of the need for women's labour as well as for ideological reasons, it is taken for granted that able women work outside the house. Indeed, in the Soviet Union, most families would be in financial difficulty without the woman's salary (Sacks, 1976, pp. 36–7; see also McAuley, 1979, p. 82). The implications of these differences are far from fully understood. Western observers interested in changing women's roles and new forms of work and family life, social scientists as well as others, all too often dismiss the massive participation of women in the labour force in Eastern Europe as a change of little consequence for the position of women in marriage and the family. Emancipation at work is said to go along with traditional family patterns so that women are simply saddled with the full burden of housework in addition to their work responsibilities outside the house. While some research has been taken to confirm this view, it is unlikely to present a full and balanced picture. A traditional division of labour in the family may persist in large parts of Eastern European societies, reinforced perhaps by earlier differences in the inherited patterns of the roles of men and women (Sokolowska, 1965, for Poland); yet it seems extremely implausible to assume that full participation of women in the labour force as well as the legitimation of women's work and the change in women's general status that tend to go with such participation, should have no impact on relations in the family. Especially among the younger generation, I expected to find new forms of division of labour between husband and wife in the dual-career families of my Eastern European respondents. Historically, developments in family life took a course in Russia and the Soviet Union that is very different from Western Europe and the United States. The traditional family system of Tsarist Russia was highly patriarchal. Ideologically, the goals of the socialist legislation after 1917 were to emancipate women and to free family relations from material calculation (Kollontai, 1926/1975). Often interpreted as a policy hostile to the family, the early Soviet legislation may be better understood as an experiment in letting forms develop without regard for traditional conventions and religious rules, an experiment that resulted in new family patterns in line with modern and changing circumstances (Koenig 1946, pp. 132–64).

In complex later developments which included reversals of policy and new starts, three factors seem to be especially important: goals of sexual equality and emancipation partly coincided and partly were at odds with economic policies maximizing labour force utilization. At the same time, the burdens which limited economic prosperity imposed on private households fell to a large extent on women and made changes in the sexual division of labour more difficult. (On this history, see Lapidus, 1978; Atkinson, Dallin and Lapidus (eds.), 1977.)

After two generations, the outcome of these changes appears to be a structure of marriage and family life that is basically similar to that of Western countries. This broad generalization disregards differences in cultural style, somewhat more austere sexual mores, the different role of religion and of the state in people's lives as well as the contrasts in standard of living and the work participation of women. However, the separation of the spheres of family and work life, changes in the composition and the size of families, and a greater emphasis on personal relations between spouses and parents and children are all developments that made life in the urban Soviet family similar to family life as we know it in Western societies (cf. Juviler, 1966; Geiger, 1965; the review of literature by Dunn and Dunn, 1977). This similarity is also expressed in an increasing frequency of divorce.[9]

Through the interviews with Eastern European professionals I sought to explore whether there is something about socialist values, the emphasis on co-operation in socialist societies, and their different organization of work and rewards which changes the impact of work pressures on relationships in marriage and friendship. This comparative exploration has no foregone conclusions. On the one hand, some may argue that American capitalist society gives more leeway to individual variation and freedom, that it gives more space to private life and thus would constitute a better environment for meaningful and fulfilled personal relations. On the other hand, socialist values and a more secure organization of economic life mitigate ambitions and pressures of work and thus give more protection to personal relations from interferences caused by these tensions and strains. However, I do not make it an unexamined assumption that because socialist education emphasizes co-operation, there is no competition and because there is job security, there are no competitive pressures. It is possible, for example, that scarce opportunities in higher education create sharp competition in school despite an emphasis on co-operation, or that participation in and dependence on large bureaucracies create more tension for the professional and set up greater expectations for conformity to organizational norms that he or she would have to cope with practising a profession independently.

There are certain difficulties of life of Eastern Europe which have nothing to do with work pressures but which may add to the strains of people's lives. I am thinking of such things as the shortage of housing, the lack of decent kindergartens in certain neighbourhoods, combined with the economic necessity of outside work for all adults, and the long waits for food. I know that there is no sure way of distinguishing the impact of these difficulties from that of work-related pressures. Nevertheless, I hoped that I could find out how my respondents perceive those different interrelationships, how they feel about the effects of different strains and difficulties, and where they identify the sources of the major tensions affecting their personal life.

Work in the Soviet Union and the German Democratic Republic

Assessments of the structure of occupations and privilege in the Soviet Union and in the German Democratic Republic tend to vary with the political inclinations of the observer. The pictures given range from state capitalism with poor, still oppressed workers whose condition did not substantially improve after the revolution, to an egalitarian society in which all workers live in a virtual paradise, no longer hampered by an exploiting political-economic regime. I looked at the environment of work for both men and women as a background to my talks. In particular, I was interested in the following issues: the special position of professionals, who are the subjects of my study; the position of women in the professions; the continuing discussion on equality in socialist societies; the variety of socio-economic supports for working men and women, and, finally, the role of ambition and competitiveness among professionals in socialist countries.

The position of professionals

As suggested earlier, professionals are less alienated than other workers; these non-alienating aspects of work are shared by professionals in both socialist and capitalist societies. Although professionals in Eastern Europe are economically not as privileged as their counterparts in Western Europe and in this country, there have been conflicts in some of the socialist countries about pay differentials for professional workers; engineers and others with technical or managerial expertise claim that since they have more responsibility they should be paid more, that there should be greater differences between their salaries and the salaries of other workers. Problems of remuneration aside, there is no question that professionals play crucial roles in any modern society because of the importance of expertise in various technologies, in management and in human services (Parkin, 1971, pp. 137–85).

Professionals in the German Democratic Republic and the Soviet Union have a greater sense of employment security than their counterparts in the United States. Even though the unemployment of professionals in the West is low, the threat is there for many, especially in the private, profit-oriented sectors of the economy. These differences seem especially pronounced in the early stages of the professional career.

Pressures and tensions are, however, persistent problems in socialist countries, too. Highly skilled engineers and other professionals reported that although they collectively decided on the time a project was to be completed, they nevertheless felt very pressured to keep that projected deadline in order not to disturb other projects that were dependent on theirs. The burden of meeting set deadlines and producing good work is especially great for top-level managers. Despite the concern for a more humane atmosphere at work, they carry heavy responsibilities for making sure their organizations do well. Not only do the workers depend on reaching production quotas for premiums added on to their regular salaries, but managers want to keep their positions, which pay comparatively well, and carry a variety of privileges. 'In both countries [United States and Soviet Union] management is a high-pressure game. Delegation of authority is an ideal on which all can agree, but the forty-hour week for managers still awaits an organizational revolution' (Granick, 1960, p. 129).

The position of women in the professions
According to socialist theory, the woman cannot participate on an equal basis either in the society or in the family unless she is part of the world of work. The ideal socialist family is based on human affection rather than on economic dependence and material interests. The hope for creating a new kind of family combined with the need for the participation of women in the labour force led to great changes in the roles of women. In the German Democratic Republic and the Soviet Union the vast majority of men and women work outside the home. 'In the Soviet Union 88 per cent of women of working age are gainfully employed, nearly all full-time or students; in East Germany 79 per cent, of whom one-third have three quarter jobs' (Mandel, 1975, p. 322). Both East German and Soviet women participate fully in professional life [10] although their distribution in different fields is not the same as that of men. Table 1.1 shows the proportion of women in three professions in several countries, including the German Democratic Republic and the Soviet Union. In the German Democratic Republic, female university students in large numbers choose literature and languages. Those who graduate from professional school fill 80 per cent of all positions in the cultural and educational fields. However, among those university and professional school graduates who are younger than thirty years, women represent more than a third in every field except technology, where they still constitute only 10–20 per cent (Menschik and Leopold, 1974, p. 88).

TABLE 1.1   *Women in selected professions, by country**

Country	Occupation (percentage)		
	Lawyers	Physicians	Dentists
US	3.5	6.5	2.1
USSR	36.0	75.0†	83.0
UK	3.8 (barristers)	16.0	6.9
Japan	3.0	9.3	3.0
Sweden	6.1	15.4	24.4
Germany (Fed. Rep.)	5.5	20.0	14.0
Germany (Dem. Rep.)	30.0	36.0	24.7
Italy	2.8	4.9	n.a.
India	0.7	9.5	3.9
Denmark	n.a.	16.4	70.0
Poland	18.8	36.4	77.0

* Most of the data in this table were brought together by Cynthia F. Epstein from a variety of sources. See her *Woman's Place* (Berkeley: University of California Press, 1971) p. 12. Jutta Menschik and Evelyn Leopold added the data for dentists in East and West Germany and for physicians in East Germany. See *Gretchens Rote Schwestern* (*Gretchen's Red Sisters*), (Frankfurt am Main: Fischer Taschenbuch Verlag, 1974) p. 23.
† It is interesting with regard to physicians that 'the effort to improve the quality of training and medical care in recent years and the increase in pay have been associated with a decline in the proportion of women in the medical profession in the Soviet Union . . . Current medical enrollments are 54 per cent female' (Lapidus, 1978, p. 188.)

In both the Soviet Union and the German Democratic Republic women are under-represented in leadership positions.

It is true that [in the GDR] 25 per cent of the directors of school are women, 13 per cent of the mayors of cities, 36 per cent of the legal leadership, 44 per cent of the union leadership, however, in industry, only every eleventh leadership position is occupied by a woman (Menschik and Leopold, 1974, p. 88).

Part of the problems women have in being appointed and elected to leadership positions relate to their traditional roles within the family. While the issues of leadership positions for women in socialist countries go beyond the limits of this study, my exploration of the difficulties in integrating work and family life will provide some insight into the problems women have who aspire to these positions.[11]

The issue of equality

If the orthodox Marxist definition of class is used to look at such Eastern European countries as the Soviet Union and East Germany, then there are virtually no antagonistic social classes because there is no ownership of the means of production and the property-owning classes have practically ceased to exist. If classes are, however, simply social strata with different levels of advantage and privilege, then there are, of course, classes in socialist societies, too. In an article written nearly twenty-five years ago, Alex Inkeles divides Soviet society into ten 'social-class groups' based on occupation, income, possession of power and authority, as well as prestige (Inkeles, 1966, pp. 516–26).

In both socialist and capitalist countries, occupation is a major determinant of power, economic advantage, and prestige in the community; it greatly affects one's class position. In Eastern Europe, although many of the derivatives of occupation, such as income, life chances, prestige and life style continue to be differentially distributed, the differentials have been reduced, thus weakening class divisions.[12] Highly skilled workers may have better wages and greater prestige than many white-collar employees. Many consider, however, inequalities of power and influence as the most important inequalities in socialist societies; these, too, are to some extent associated with occupation. Being a member of the intelligentsia, then, still brings many advantages.

Children know they have to work very hard to get into institutions of learning and since in the Soviet Union there are fewer openings than applicants in the university, there is great competition to get in.

The growth of the competitive pressures can be seen in the admission statistics reported for the 1972/73 academic year. Only 22 per cent of secondary school graduates could enter day time higher education. This may be contrasted to 25 per cent in 1960, 50 per cent in 1950, and 80 per cent in 1940 (Lipset, 1973, p. 359).

In the Soviet Union, children of intellectuals tend to do better in school and have a greater chance of being accepted into university than the children of workers and peasants. Table 1.2 shows the broad social backgrounds of students in higher education. Table 1.3 shows for one province the different

TABLE 1.2 *Social groups and the VUZ (Higher Educational Institution) student body*, circa *1964*

| Social groups* | % of total population | % of VUZ student body† | | |
		Full-time courses	Evening courses	Correspondence courses
Employees	21.0	41.0	47.1	67.3
Workers	54.1	39.4	50.6	25.7
Peasants	24.8	19.6	2.3	7.0

* *Narodnoe khozyaistvo SSSR v* (1964) p. 33. The figure for "employees" is an approximation for all workers of predominantly mental labour. Private peasants and craftsmen now comprised only 0.1 per cent of the population.

† E. L. Manevich, *Problemy obshchestvennogo truda v SSSR* (Moscow, 1966) p. 63.

SOURCE Mervyn Matthews, *Class and Society* (New York: Walker, 1972) p. 297.

TABLE 1.3 *Admissions to first-year day-time divisions of Sverdlovsk higher educational institutions, 1968, according to social origin*

| Higher educational institutions | | Social origin (in %) | | |
	Total	Workers	Employees	Collective farmers
Pedagogical institute	783	41.8	56.2	2.0
Institute of national economy	525	49.5	47.3	3.2
University	600	43.7	52.5	3.8
Juridical institute	500	43.0	44.2	12.8
Agricultural institute	325	43.1	22.5	34.4
Medical institute	500	26.8	72.0	1.2
Railroad institute	575	58.7	39.2	2.1
Lumber technical institute	900	49.8	47.0	3.2
Polytechnical institute	2 250	34.1	64.4	1.5
Mining institute	850	62.6	37.0	0.4
Total	**7 808**	**43.5**	**52.1**	**4.4**

SOURCE M. N. Rutkevich and F. R. Filippov, 'Social Sources of Recruitment of the Intelligentsia', in Murray Yanowich and Wesley A. Fisher, (eds), *Social Stratification and Mobility in the U.S.S.R.* (New York: International Arts and Science Press, 1973) p. 250.

institutes the students enter and the percentages of children of workers, employees and collective farmers within each institute. In the German Democratic Republic, there has been an effort to have more children of workers in higher institutions of learning. For many years, it was difficult for the children of the 'middle class' to be accepted. All children know, however, they must work hard to pass the examinations. If they take a trade and decide later on to improve their qualifications and enter a professional field, there are many possibilities for attending university full-time or doing part-time studies.

In 1967, 38.2 per cent of the students attending university in the German Democratic Republic came from workers' families (Menschik and Leopold, 1974, p. 64). East German policies encouraging children from workers' families were designed to counteract an extreme situation inherited from the past. In 1928–9 the share of workers' children was only 2.2 per cent (Rueschemeyer, 1973, p. 220).

By comparison, Blau and Duncan (1967, pp. 39 and 496) show that in the United States 37 per cent of all professionals and 22 per cent of self-employed professionals had fathers in blue-collar occupations. As impressive as these figures appear, especially in view of the somewhat smaller size of the American working class, one has to bear in mind that the American definition of professional is wider than the categories of occupations requiring higher education used in the European studies.

Socio-economic supports for working men and women
Socialist societies, though lower in production than Western capitalist countries, use a large proportion of the national income for public services and economic guarantees. Medical and educational programmes, the security of work, the various legal rights of working women, concrete supports in child care, are later discussed in detail. These supports are crucial for feelings of confidence for both men and women. They know that there is a level below which they cannot fall, even if the practical strains of accomplishing what they want to do are great.

Ambition and competitiveness
After it became clear from my first interviews with professionals in the United States that ambition and competitiveness were of

great importance for the ways in which work pressures affect personal relations outside work, I sought to develop some hypotheses about the intensity of ambition among professionals in socialist societies. One early limitation Soviet students face is that some courses of study in higher institutions of learning are in effect closed because there is need for only a limited number of practitioners. American students face similar problems, though they are able to continue studying without work guarantees and, in some fields, promising career prospects. The Soviet students must choose areas of study where they can find employment afterwards.

Is it true that because men and women grew up with socialist values in school, because they are given many supports and especially because they enjoy a high degree of job security, an atmosphere at work develops which is different from the one American professionals describe? A positive answer is not obvious. Education in school seeks to further co-operative attitudes, but political socialization, while effective to an extent, is not without limitations (Brown and Gray (eds), 1977; White, 1979). In addition, diminished inequalities of educational opportunity are bound to increase competition in the years of one's life when access to higher and professional education is at stake. Furthermore, the socialist leadership and managers at various levels invoke ideological commitments, set ambitious targets and promise honours in order to increase voluntary effort and achievement. *Leistungsdruck* (pressure to perform) in this sense is an issue in the German Democratic Republic as well as in other socialist societies. The development of personal ambition is, of course, a very complicated issue and only in part determined by the patterns of opportunity and the political and cultural atmosphere in which one lives. On balance, however, I expected to find among the professionals in the socialist societies a lower level of work pressure and its internalized variant, ambition. Two observations may be quoted to illustrate this hypothesis: The first is by an executive in the chemistry and plastics industry:

> People value the security of this system . . . the state honors and remunerates the hard worker, but it also protects the one who cannot or does not work hard. Businessmen have asked me why I don't flee to the Federal Republic where I would be offered a position that pays ten to twenty times what I earn

here. Frankly, I'm afraid I might not make out in the harried, hurried competitive jungle of the capitalist world. And if I did, at what price? Our tempo is slower, we take it easier. True, maybe this lack of competitive pressure and initiative has kept us behind, but I wouldn't want to change my job for a similar one in West Germany (Dornberg, 1968, pp. 22–3).

Another insight comes from a young man who emigrated from the German Democratic Republic to West Germany. Although he talks about workers, the yearnings he senses are not restricted to one social group.

The people in the neighbourhood where my parents live are all miners. One can never break out – socialist society doesn't grant that possibility. One can study or become something else but not break out. Here [in West Germany] every man has in his unconscious the hope to make something out of his life. There are practically no apprentices in small shops who don't dream about being self-employed. The ambition is a dividing factor. Ambition in the German Democratic Republic is limited. Here in the West, when a worker has saved 2000 marks he can travel to the Sudan and shoot a deer. That is alienation in our society; the worker believes he is no longer a worker. There, the worker sees himself very clearly as a worker, he is the basis of the state, he has changed the society (Grunert-Bronnen, 1970, p. 115).

In the following chapters, then, I will discuss the effects of work-related pressures and ambitions on personal relations, especially marital relations. Though important for a thorough understanding of work, family and personal life in modern societies, these problems have remained largely ignored as far as empirical sociological research, in contrast to philosophical critique, is concerned. Going beyond conditions in the United States, I tried to explore how socialist values, the emphasis on co-operation, and the different organization of work and its rewards in socialist societies affect the interrelations between work and personal life outside work. Here the basic question is to what extent these societies have succeeded in reducing the alienation which, according to Marx, is inherent in capitalist society. In both settings, I have focused on professionals because this makes the investigations of these countries more comparable and because professional work raises especially interesting questions about the interrelations between work and personal life.

The second major concern of this study is the effect of the participation of women in the professions on their self-conceptions and on their personal relationships. In particular, I am interested in some of the consequences of increasing equality between men and women for their relations in marriage. I explore these questions by comparing families in which only the husband works outside the house with those in which both spouses participate in the world of work.

This investigation had to limit itself to the perceptions, memories and interpretations of the people I interviewed. However, the present understanding of the problems discussed is such that a qualitative exploration of people's own interpretations seems the best way of developing insights and hypotheses; that, rather than the testing of pre-formulated assumptions is what I want to do.

Chapter 2 deals with the effects of work demands on families where only the husband practises his profession. Chapter 3 discusses dual-career families in America. Chapter 4 presents the materials on dual-career professional families in the Soviet Union and the German Democratic Republic, and the book concludes with a comparative discussion in Chapter 5.

2 'No, my wife doesn't work – she's a housewife': American single-career families

Introduction

In this chapter, I focus on professional men whose wives stay at home and on 'at home' wives married to professionals. The effects of work tensions on family relationships are discussed separately for men and women in order to give emphasis to the special perspective of each group. These differences are more acute in the single-career families than in those families where both husbands and wives practise professionally because of the contrasting daily experiences of the men and women and the greater separation of roles. The woman at home is most affected by disturbances in the marriage (Goode, 1964). Psychologically and materially, she is dependent on that relationship; often she has no outside involvements to relieve the strains at home. In turn, her reactions to this situation influence the development of the marriage.

In my interviews I focused, firstly, on the work situation and the work pressures of the professionals as perceived by both 'at home' wives and by the professionals themselves. Secondly, I explored how the men's attitudes and ambitions towards their work relate to their upbringing and education. Thirdly, I tried to understand how the men and women see the effects of these pressures not only on their personality and personal development but on their marriage and friendships.

I interviewed ten men and ten women. Each interview lasted about two hours. The talks with the women took place at home; I spoke with most of the men at home or at work. At the end of this chapter is the interview guide I used. There are also notes on my experience during the interviews which reveal some of my personal reactions to the men and women I spoke with, as well as to the interview guide itself.

23

The men ranged in age from thirty to fifty-two; their wives were either the same age or two to three years younger than their husbands. The range for the women I spoke with was approximately the same. All the respondents had children. Table 2.1 shows the age and position of the men I spoke with. All the male respondents had post-graduate degrees in their fields. Eight of their wives worked outside the home until their first pregnancy; their positions and educational background are shown in Table 2.2.

Most of the women I spoke with had finished college; since the birth of their children, however, who were generally still of

TABLE 2.1   *Age and position of male respondents*

Age	Position
33	Assistant professor – social sciences
30	Psychiatrist working in a private hospital and lecturing at a medical school
34	Psychiatrist in private practice
35	Associate professor – natural sciences
41	Scientist – public research organization
47	Engineer – high-level position in private industry
48	Physician with medical administrative duties
48	President of a large business organization
49	Lawyer in private practice
52	Physician in private practice

TABLE 2.2   *Wives' positions before pregnancy and present educational background*

Position before pregnancy	Educational background
Editor of a trade journal	BA
Designer	BA
Social worker	BA
Did not work after marriage outside house	Law degree
Landscape designer	BSc
Elementary school teacher	BA
Elementary school teacher	MA
Secretary	Has recently started college (part-time)
Secretary	Did not finish college
Did not work outside home	Did not finish college

TABLE 2.3 *Education and family background of the women respondents*

Education and major subject	Father's education	Mother's education	Father's occupation	Mother's occupation
BA French	Law degree	BA	Lawyer	
BA Sociology	MA	BA	Principal	High-school teacher (after the children were in school full-time)
Art school	Elementary school	Elementary	Small businessman	
BA Music	Medical degree	BS	Doctor	Labouratory assistant (after the children were in their teens)
BA French	BS	Teacher's college	Engineer	Elementary school teacher (before children were born)
Nursing degree	High school	High school – incomplete	Carpenter – contractor	Book-keeper and librarian after children were in school
BA Dance MA Remedial reading	College – 2 years	High school	Party functionary, organization fund-raiser	Secretary – after children were in school
College – 2 years	medical degree	High school	Doctor	–
BA Retailing	High school – incomplete	High school – incomplete	Assistant manager of a small business enterprise	–
BA History	BS	College–two years	Civil engineer	Secretary – before the children were born

TABLE 2.4   *Professions of the husbands of 'at home' wives*

Professions
Lecturer in the social sciences – still in graduate school
Assistant professor in the social sciences
Assistant professor in the natural sciences; director of a major national research project
Professor in liberal arts
Doctor in private practice with a part-time teaching position in a medical school
Two high-level medicine administrators
Lawyer in private practice
Management consultant in private practice
Pension consultant in private practice

elementary school age at the time of our talks, they had not worked outside the house. Table 2.3 gives a more detailed picture of their education and family background. The positions of their husbands are shown in Table 2.4. When I started the interviewing, four of the women I spoke with had just begun part-time work or study. One very interesting finding was that these four women had mothers who worked outside the house while they still lived at home; all of the other women in this group had mothers who remained at home while they were growing up.

The work situation

The long hours of work described by the wives of professionals were confirmed by the men I spoke with. Even if one suspects some exaggeration, the hours most of these professionals work are extraordinary. One natural scientist said that he never slept more than six hours a night and sometimes only four. He works all the time, evenings and weekends as well, when he has a chance. The self-employed physician usually works seventy hours a week; the engineer said he worked twenty-five hours a day. After dinner, most professionals continue their work at home or leave to see patients, teach or attend business or community meetings. A few maintain this schedule every day; the others, two or three times a week. There was not one professional, however, who did not return a few evenings during the month or on a Saturday morning to complete some unfinished business or to take care of patients in the hospital. Most took a couple of hours off on Sunday to do something with the children; with the medical administrators, scientists and engineer, even that could not be taken for granted. One woman said of her husband, 'If he has five minutes free, he'll run into the study to work.' In addition, several of the professionals did extensive travelling; one was able to take his wife on these trips, the other three usually travelled alone. One scientist was away for fifteen weeks even during his sabbatical year. The medical administrator said he spent 25 per cent of his time out of town, an indication, according to him, of how good his department is. The engineer described a working period three years ago where he kept taking a week's trip every six weeks. As one wife said of her husband, 'He is always running.'

Two of the professionals with extremely long hours said they came home for dinner in order to eat with the children, one because his wife 'insists on it'. The lawyers and the psychiatrist in private practice had the least demanding schedules, only occasionally having to be out in the evenings.

Most of the professionals exercised a great deal of authority at work, with considerable control over people, power to make decisions affecting the lives of the people who worked with them, and great feelings of personal responsibility for the success of their organization. When the professionals did not have the authority they thought they were entitled to, some changed their work setting. For example, the psychiatrist working in an institutional setting changed to private practice; the doctor trying to build up a general practice changed to a more specific clientele. He described the reasons for this change:

I was disappointed with the practice of medicine. My patients were demanding; they shopped around and made demands. The rich think you're a slave. They demand you come. Medicine is no longer a prestigious profession. . . . Thousands of people who were poor never got treatment. They appreciate me; they're respectful. . . . While I'm away in the summer, the loyal ones wait, even at some risk to themselves. . . . My patients worship me.

While the few who continue to be in a position with less authority than they think they should have experience tensions in this aspect of their work lives, so do those in positions of great authority. These tensions will be discussed in the next section. The lawyers had, perhaps, the most comfortable relationships at work. Each of the partners specialized in different aspects of the law, giving each one some authority. Many of the decisions involving office administration as well as relationships with clients were made in common: 'We pay attention to the other person's point of view.' Sharing of authority is not peculiar to the work situation of the lawyer. Most of the other professionals also work in colleague groups where authority is shared and decisions are made in common; however, often these groups are only part of a larger set of relations in their organization.

Sources of tensions at work

Early socialization into the profession is a preparation for future time demands, continual performance evaluation and expected social, political and occupational attitudes of the professional worker. Some of this training for professional work has begun early in the child's life, continuing on in professional school. The 'culmination', however, is early practice. Early practice is in many ways a critical period. The first experience of 'real work' comes together with the effort to prove oneself. There is some evidence that attitudes formed and reshaped in this period last long into later years.

Not unexpectedly, the men I spoke with found this period to be an extremely difficult one. For many, the time demands alone were extraordinary. They were the most intense for doctors: 'At first, I worked hard to be accepted into the hospital. I worked nights and weekends. I would go anywhere and at any time to see the patients.' Academics, however, soon catch up with them. After an initial period of relief after the completion of the Ph.D. and success in finding a satisfactory position, the new instructor usually concentrates on teaching, preparing his classes well and maintaining good relationships with his students – important criteria, he is told, for promotion and tenure. This initial period, of course, is not without tension; the young teacher is very concerned about his performance. The academic soon finds out, however, if he is not aware of it before, that he is judged by other criteria, which are equally, if not even more crucial for his future career development. This realization leads him not only to spend evenings and weekends working but creates a whole set of uncertainties and tensions. It is interesting that although none of the wives of the academics without tenure thought their husbands were competitive people, they believed other young people in the department were terribly concerned about the problem, talking about it all the time or, in the case of some, 'buttering up the chairman'.

The young academic is expected to publish a sufficient amount and publish in the right journals if he wants tenure; the psychiatrist in the mental hospital has to continue to do his research and publish in order to maintain his affiliation with the university. Often, young people are included in committee positions with administrative responsibilities. Still, they are expected to do their research and publish. The reaction, according to the men I spoke with, is not only tension because of unreasonable time demands but insecurity about what really is important for promotion and concern about the probability of fulfilling all these expectations. 'When I was advisor I had no time . . . I had to maintain my level. It was bad when I went to the lab. six nights a week. My wife was alone six nights a week. . . . She realized I had to do it.' (Scientist)

Compounding the academic's worries about his insecure position are the important social relationships which take place in the department. How much is one judged by 'objective' criteria?

It took time to understand academic politics and one's social-professional relationships. These are connected to each other. . . . How one gets along is important, how one impresses other people. You must have a patron. You have to find out who has the power. There are factions; it's hard to know everyone. Some who hardly come in are the most important. . . . I began to go to faculty meetings and observe where people sat. (Social scientist)

A few of the men complained of having to socialize with their colleagues:

People don't want to talk about their fields but give the impression that what they are doing is important. (Social scientist)

My colleagues go to all the social functions and dress properly. My self-image isn't that way. I don't see myself as a great success and that's society's image of a man. (Scientist–public industry)

The president of the large business organization spoke of the importance of one's circle of friends for advancement in the organization. 'At one point, there was intense competition between several men; two of us had college degrees. I got the position. I travelled in the right social circles. It is very helpful to do so.'

Incorporating the different criteria of advancement is seen by many of the professionals as just 'learning to play the game'. One academic, however, continued to work only on the improvement of his formal, academic credentials. 'I tried harder and harder to establish an objective record. I worked longer and longer hours.'

At the beginning of one's career, the salient question is whether or not one is able to remain in the organization at all and even at a later stage, this may be a problem for the professional. 'I feel insecure but don't think too much about it. I could get a job if I were willing to move. It's not easy. I'm in my forties and don't have many publications. I'm competing with younger people who have published more.' (Scientist) Those who are defined as not making it may experience not only extreme anxiety about the future but, in addition, may be isolated from their colleagues. 'I reacted with isolation and anxiety. You're not invited, even when a visiting scholar in your field comes. People drop you because you're not going anywhere in the department. As soon as they become aware of it, they stop bothering with you.' (Social scientist)

Loss, however, should be taken with grace; a smiling face keeps up the impression that things are working smoothly, that there are no knots in the system. 'When he didn't get the promotion, he was disappointed but didn't show it and congratulated me. . . . Even when people were running for the top job, they were friendly.' (President–large organization)

Most of those who fail still believe in the fairness of the system; they recognize its legitimacy and often blame themselves for not doing better.

I'm held back by my———problem. I've taken courses and

gone to therapy but I don't do the exercises. It's my fault. It took me years to share the problem with my wife.

In 197–, I was passed over and didn't become the manager. I was severely depressed and had to go into therapy. Afterwards, the organization supported me. I feel well regarded now; then I felt like a failure.

The same high-level engineer described his job in the broader context of private industry. He found the use of hard business tactics reasonable and explained the move of the defence industry out of 'house', out of government supported projects into private industry: 'If it's government supported, there's a fixed overhead. In industry, if you don't need a project any more, there are no qualms in terminating it. It's easier for private industry to fire someone.'

Even if one's job is secure, there is competition in both public and private organizations about other matters. This is especially important in the later stages of the career. In academic work, extensive publishing improves the professional's chances of getting a higher salary, and promotion. It brings him into contact with other established people in his field and increases his reputation as well as his self-esteem. This competition is quite intense. Among the natural scientists, it may lead to a reluctance to share one's ideas with any but a selected, trusted group of people.

You would not talk extensively about a problem you are working on with strangers. It may not work out; they may finish it off. I talk to everyone in my department but one summer I worked with someone from another university here and he went back and wrote the research up and published it. I thought he was my friend. Later, he kept calling and calling, he felt so guilty. He suffered as much as I did.

Sometimes, people don't want to share a half-baked idea but sometimes they are petty and over-guarded. I've seen cases in departments where people brought law suits against each other. In one department, when a senior person works on a paper with a younger colleague, he insists on having his name first even if he hardly did any of the work.

The competition takes place at different levels. It may be a competition with others outside one's own organization and even benefit the immediate colleagues, although even then, success and failure affect one's standing among the colleagues. Thus, academics are often pressured to compete for outside funding.

The school is poor. I have to get one third of my salary through grants. If I don't get it, I'm not fired but then some younger person has to go. I also support students. The pressure is subtle. Every year, I have to apply again. I leave my ego out because I know how these decisions are made. (Associate professor – natural sciences)

In public industry, supervisors have to apply for project funds. 'The pentagon gives money through several different groups which fund various projects.' (Scientist) In both private and public industry, there is strong competition for funding: 'In order to remain alive, we have to be competitive, to produce ideas. Otherwise, we have to go out of business. People value our technical contributions. We also have to be cost conscious. The managers beat on us to show profit.' (Engineer – private industry)

Competition that takes place within one's organization and even one's immediate work group may be muffled and modified in form by the necessity of working together, by courtesy and friendship; it is nevertheless pervasive, according to the men and women I spoke with. The professionals both in public and private institutions take for granted that people will push for their own interests. Groups working in one institution compete for resources within that institution. In academic departments, some people want to do their own research and otherwise not waste their time making any contributions to the department. They become involved only when their own interests are threatened.

Even people who by any standard have 'made it' are not immune from tensions. Aside from the extraordinary hours they work and their reluctance to share real problems and weaknesses with subordinates, there is a feeling they always have to be up-to-date with a wide variety of professional and organizational concerns. 'I have directors to keep track of. I always have to be prepared.' (President of large organization)

In order to advance professionally, several of the men felt they had to make compromises in personal relations or agree to decisions they did not really believe in. The moral pain may be dulled by repetition, but then it may not be. Certainly, situations involving conflicting commitments do not vanish with success. Since people in authority are in the position of affecting the lives of other human beings, they are caught between human commitments and profit – or reputational considerations. 'I don't like to tell people they're not doing well. The last director had to fire a high-level administrator and became very ill afterwards.' One high-level medical administrator suggested that these difficulties were somewhat relieved for him because of the specialization of fields of the people who worked for him and the transfer possibilities.

The contradiction between organizational interests and the interests of individuals, which comes to light in these dilemmas of top administrators, is a harsher reality for the people directly affected. Several of the men I spoke with felt that their individual interests and their needs as human beings were often not taken into consideration in the work demands made on them.

> They don't care about you. They say you are supposed to do research. They tell you to take the time from what you're doing. I can't because the patient gets cheated. . . . I guess I'm a bit idealistic and think if you act honestly, you'll get treated fairly, but it doesn't always work out.

> I was trying to do my research while having an administrative position with a large number of students under me. I did it for two years and then wanted to drop it. The chairman didn't want me to. I said I would leave.

How do the men react to their work lives? What are their present ambitions? Except for very few people, success is still to be achieved and if it is already achieved it has to be maintained. Here the past history of competitiveness and tension at work seems important for our discussion. All of these men felt intense ambition and competition in their work lives, according to their wives' responses or their own. A few had severe stomach problems in their twenties when they were 'proving themselves'. One lawyer, from law school on, competed first with other students and then until recently for clients; he was extremely tense and dissatisfied until he thought he had 'made it'. Some of the men had a history and expectation of always coming out on top. Their environment was a competitive one and their sense of what 'top' is, especially for the most successful, remains an open question. Being in very high administrative positions, could they have even more responsibility? Was it still possible to make brilliant research contributions along with administrative duties? The men seem, at times, to be actually seeking out more work. 'I do seventy miles a day at least and see three hundred and fifty patients. I want one thousand. You don't have to see them all. You can look at their records.' (Doctor) The engineer in industry who was out several evenings a week, teaching, attending community meetings and was now worried about finding the time for a chapter he volunteered to write, said frankly: 'I wouldn't want more time at home than I have.' One of the scientists felt uncomfortable when he was not working:

Sometimes if I take the time to do family things, I realize the next day I would have been better off if I hadn't. . . .We both have the work ethic. I would work hard no matter what I do – so does she. My wife can disconnect more than I can, though; she doesn't feel guilty when she takes time off.

Another professional, on top of a terribly busy schedule, took on secretarial chores for a year after his secretary became sick and her associate left.

I brought home work. After midnight, I was keeping books but the payroll was reduced by $25 000 a year . . . I had to give more time. I had a lot of bills uncollected. The cash wasn't there and that caused arguments. The calls were driving us crazy. We were fighting and angry. Finally, I got a super billing clerk.

Three professionals viewed themselves as partial failures.

Sometimes I think I would like to go into government service and carry out a large project. This company doesn't give me the chance. I have few opportunities to carry out things I initiate . . . but I have to stay and put my kids through school. (Engineer – private industry)

I would like to go up two more grades, not to become a supervisor but a consultant. (Scientist – public industry)

One scientist did not want to become a supervisor and therefore did not apply for all the positions that came up. His so-called lack of ambition influenced how others perceived him. 'I am thought of as not ambitious enough because I don't apply for all the positions that come up. Maybe I should apply. I'm expected to but they don't really fit me.' In such an environment, men feel themselves in danger of moving down the prestige ladder of an organization, if they fail or choose not to try for a position of higher rank than they already have. Only one of the professionals vaguely thought of starting a new and quieter life for himself in a small town; the others did not speak of such alternatives. Two of the men, the lawyer and the psychiatrist in private practice, did not appear to be overwhelmed by an open-ended ambition; they seemed to be content with what they were doing. This may be largely due to the fact that self-employed professionals are not faced with organizational careers and normally do not directly compete with each other for fame.

Background of the professionals

How and when did the strong ambitions and competitive feelings develop? While I cannot hope to explore the internal relationships in the family which might have encouraged such a development, most of my respondents indicated that a general push to achieve was present even in the earliest years.

From the beginning, I was programmed to be a pro-fessional . . . a teacher, doctor, lawyer or priest. I was pushed into it. My father was a teacher in high school. . . . I had an obligation to work from the very beginning. Just working for fun hasn't happened yet. (Psychiatrist)

The work ethic was more ingrained in me by my family than it is in other people. I started to work pumping gas, etc. when I was twelve, after school and on vacations. I've never stopped working since. (President of organization)

Table 2.5 summarizes the educational background and pro-fession of the male respondents' parents. More than half of these men, as well as half of the husbands of the women I interviewed,

TABLE 2.5 Education and profession of men's parents in single-career families

Respondent's profession	Education of father	Occupation of father	Education of mother	Occupation of mother
Assistant professor – social sciences	High school – incomplete	Owned small shop	High school incomplete	Worked in shop
Psychiatrist hospital	Medical degree	Doctor	College	Elementary school teacher before children were born; substituted occasionally afterwards
Psychiatrist – private practice	College	High school teacher	College	Elementary school teacher; taught before children were born and after they were out of high school
Associate professor – natural sciences	High school	Federal conservation aide	High school – incomplete	Clerk in a department store after the children completed high school
Scientist – public research organization	High school – incomplete	Butcher	High school – incomplete	Worked as a clerk when children were in high school
Engineer – high-level position in private industry	High school	Owned small greengrocer's shop	High school – incomplete	Worked in greengrocer's
Physician with medical administrative duties	High school – incomplete	Poet, principal of a parochial elementary school	College	Did not work outside the house after the children were born
President of a large business organization	College – incomplete	President of a manufacturing company	College	Did not work outside the house
Lawyer in private practice	High school	Owned wholesale grocery store	High school – incomplete	Worked in store
Physician in practice	High school	Merchant, real estate broker	Post-graduate degree	Owned business

were upwardly mobile. The women I spoke with said that their husbands' families pushed the children to work hard, that as far back as they had heard about it, the children worked hard and did well in school. One man, who had been raised 'on the other side of town', his wife suggested, had never got over it. His wife thought her husband's own family was never satisfied with what they achieved, always wanting more. As a teenager, he told her that he could not stand his peers in school 'living in houses with trimmed bushes and wearing argyle socks' and then compare his situation to theirs.

A few of the professionals had parents who were immigrants and did not have the possibility of finishing even high school in the United States. Even those parents who themselves were successful in America had high ambitions for their children.

I always worked hard. Excellence was demanded. My parents sent us to college to do well – they paid a fortune. All the children went to college and have college degrees. They got them whether they liked it or not. After the third year, when I hesitated about going back, my mother said she'd beat me with a broom all the way to Cambridge. My parents never let up, my mother particularly.

This rather powerful mother went to professional school herself in her thirties while there were several children at home; later on, she made a fortune in business.

It would be inaccurate to suggest that strong achievement orientation exists only where there is considerable social mobility. Some of the women whose husbands were born into the upper middle class perceived their husbands as men who even as adolescents worked hard, intending to excel. One wife, whose father-in-law was a successful professional, said her husband's mother was always dissatisfied and continually pressured everyone in the family to perform better. This woman later committed suicide, and her daughter who had been as upset about the death as the son also attempted suicide a few years ago.

Ambitious tendencies developed in the family are channelled in definite ways in the school system and even children not coming from particularly ambitious families are affected by these.

The schooling of American professional men

For all of the professionals, school happened a long time ago and although present interpretations of the past are problematical, I was not interested in objective truths but the feelings and reactions of the people I spoke with. None of the men mentioned the opening of intellectual worlds at school or friendships that developed with classmates, even though I asked them to think about what they found to be particularly good as well as particularly painful experiences in their years of schooling.

Except for one professional who had been held back in kindergarten, most memories of school started with high school. One of the psychiatrists was accused of cheating because he did homework with a friend; many children have had similar experiences in school, experiences which discourage co-operation. 'I sat and did homework with a friend in high school and then was told my honours would be taken away from me for that period because we cheated. I didn't think I cheated but I believed in the teacher's reality.' (Psychiatrist) Two of the negative experiences of the professionals revolved around the traditional approach to the material; however the worst experiences at school were failures to achieve what the students hoped for.

In my school, there were six prizes for those with the highest standing and I came in seventh. I was disappointed. It seemed to be an arbitrary decision. It made me think, however, that these grades didn't have such a relationship to achievement. Many of us made it into Harvard. (Social scientist)

In the eighth grade, I was elected president of the class, in the next year as well. The third year, I didn't make it. I guess I thought I'd just continue on . . . I was also disappointed I didn't get a letter on the baseball team. (President of large organization)

From the very beginning of school, certain children knew they were going to do well. Competition was by no means limited but they had a secure position with respect to many other children and that made competition easier to take.

Even in high school, peer groups established themselves as

being better or worse . . . in grammar school, too. (Engineer)

I always enjoyed competition. I went to a rural high school and got A's and B's without working hard. The last year, eight of us sat down and learned geometry together. Our teacher let us play around and experiment in the laboratory. (Associate professor – natural sciences)

The concern with achieving became even more intense in college.

When I got into college, we were told only one out of three students graduated. My parents weren't well-to-do. I decided I wouldn't flunk out and worked like hell. There were guys who sat around, drank and played cards – and accused us of being grinds. (Associate professor – natural sciences)

Not surprisingly, the students in the pre-medical programme had the worst experiences:

We compared grades. If you asked someone to do something and he said he had to study, you wondered if you should, too. People cheated on tests; they rarely studied together. (Psychiatrist)

If you missed lectures, they wouldn't give you the notes. If other students got hold of exams from the previous year, they wouldn't share it with you. We never studied together. (Doctor)

A great problem in school was fighting for grades. In one exam, I got a good mark but because so many failed, he removed them from the curve and gave me a poor mark. This happened four or five times. The teachers were ball-busters. (Psychiatrist)

These experiences continued even in medical school, and similar pressures in their training were reported by other professionals.

They push you so hard. One professor told me that you don't know what human animals can do until you push them to the wall. There was no time to do anything else. We had a quiz every day. I often failed but I didn't miss a day so they would think I cared. I hated medicine. I wanted to drop out but I said I would stick to it. Medical school was the other side of the hell. Friends dropped out who were brighter than I was. I think other schools were better; this was a bad one.

I changed to Berkeley because there was a co-operative atmosphere which is different from Harvard. Harvard was fiercely competitive. The level of anxiety was high, the quality of our relationships was different. At Berkeley, we shared notes and had sessions together. That didn't happen at Harvard.

What did these professionals think about the pressures and the competition they experienced in their professional training?

It's natural to want to be on top. You wouldn't be human if you didn't try to do your best. I'm not shattered if I finish second or third. I needed good grades because of fellowships and job possibilities. You want to stay on top . . . but it's a healthy competition. My friend was so happy the one time he got a higher mark than I did – but we did study and help each other.

I don't have to be the only one who is tops but I have to be in the top group. In law, if you don't make the Harvard Law Review, you have no future. I went to law school for a year and finished with a solid C. Since I wasn't on top, it made me think it wasn't for me. This affects people if they're high achievers.

Slowly, but steadily, even those who were not particularly competitive said that they found themselves in situations in which they were striving to be on top. Not surprisingly, then, the most rewarding, the best remembered experiences at school were experiences of achievement, especially academic achievements, but also achievements in competitive sports.

All of these observations are based on the memories of the men I spoke with. Their concentration on achievement helped them fulfil the requirements of their schooling; at the same time, it was a preparation for their future work demands, for a nearly unlimited concentration on work goals, for tremendous time commitments, and for relegating the human concerns of friendship and co-operation to second place when professional success is at stake. For those few who had serious self-doubt in pre-professional education or even in professional school about the worth of what they were doing, the knowledge of the tremendous prestige of their profession, especially medicine, allowed them not only to live with a pressured and competitive colleague group, but even eased their acceptance of their own degradation in the classroom; anyway, if that is the way of the world, there is nothing much to do – one might as well be on top.

Effects of tensions on family relations; the wives' perspective

Nearly all the women when asked how they felt about their husbands' jobs, leaving aside for the moment positive evaluations, thought their husbands spent too much time away from home, and said that when they were home they would either continue to work too much or indicate pressures in other ways, being exhausted ('He has no more energy left for us'), not being able to unwind ('He comes home after a week at work and runs around the house immediately fixing something or paying a bill; it takes him a couple of days to be able to relax'); getting annoyed if everything in the house is not exactly on schedule or everything is not put in its proper place ('Why doesn't the house run like the ————project?'). The wife's response to the last reaction was that she could not plan her life like that with children. Another woman said that her husband sometimes gives her orders, instead of picking up a pillow or pot and putting it in its proper place.

That their husbands were moody, withdrawn or tense with the children were observations of a few of the wives but most of the women felt that the men were good fathers, interested in the children and able to concentrate on them during the few hours they were together. The wife of a doctor, whose husband was often not around, said her husband felt so guilty about not spending more time with the children that he picked on impossible times of the day to have long talks with them, for example, when the boys were getting ready for school.

For all of the women, the most intense pressures were during the periods the men were trying to 'make it', get tenure, public recognition, etc. One woman who had spent the first year of her married life in Europe with a work-absorbed husband described it this way:

> He worked night and day in the beginning. Until he was married he left everything else out. It took a long time to

persuade him to ramble in R———. When we first married, I wasn't liberated. I wouldn't go out alone but stay by myself. Back at Harvard, he worked every night until one. We became estranged; we weren't spending time knitting each other together.[1]

In this phase of establishing oneself, there are fierce pressures to finish one's thesis, to retain a job, to publish, to satisfy customers, to make a good reputation. If we think of this period as the most difficult time of one's life, we see, first of all, that it can last as long as ten years. 'When J——— finished his degree, I thought it would be my turn. I got involved politically and when I asked him to baby-sit in the evening, he would agree as long as the children were in bed first. I continued to have all the responsibility.' When the men finally became 'successful', there was much less tension at home. 'Our first years of marriage were really bad. We were fighting all the time. He was busy achieving and I was doing the shit work. We had our first kid a year and a half after we were married and had financial problems. Now he's achieved status, he has more ego.'

Recognition and security, though, do not necessarily lead to spending significantly less time at work. Only two of the eight wives whose husbands were 'successful' indicated that the husbands now take more time out to enjoy themselves and be with their families. These two women said that they pressured their husbands to do so, that the reduction of work pressure alone would not have caused the change. The assistant professor's wife who was concerned about the stability of her husband's position and the wife of the instructor still in graduate school expected the next stages of their husbands' careers (receiving the doctorate and tenure) to bring more free time and help in the family. To judge from the experiences of other wives, that may well be an illusion.[2] From the responses of the women, I could not help thinking that the husbands no longer know how *not* to work intensely. Work was the routine developed over years; the men had dropped most of their other interests and would have had to establish new patterns of behaviour in order not to fall back into their old work schedules.

How do the wives react to these working patterns of their husbands? They feel many things, some of which, not unexpectedly, contradict each other. Nine out of ten of the women (excluding the wife of the instructor still in graduate school) are most pleased with their husbands' achievements, enjoy the income and the prestige of their husbands' positions. One of the women who admitted to practically having no contact with her husband enjoyed being a VIP and having people come over to greet her. But she also said, 'Of course they are not greeting me.'

The women who saw their marriages improve over the years had husbands who did not radically change their hours but did, to some degree, change their feelings about the importance of personal relationships in their lives. One man went into group therapy after he and his wife separated and his sister developed similar problems to his. In the group, he was confronted by challenges regarding his attitude and shifting of family responsibility to his wife; his wife thought the therapy saved their marriage and the husband now made far greater efforts at home.

By far the most significant change in the marital relationship came from the influence of the Women's Movement which drastically affected eight of the ten women in their view of their situation, although only two belonged to a feminist organization. I do not think that this is an accident due to the selection of cases, although the Women's Movement probably has a lesser impact on older women and on women in some other parts of the country. One wife who had been trained as a nurse said of her encounter with the Women's Movement:

> I didn't know what to do. I thought you got married and had children, working perhaps part-time. I was happy to be at home because I didn't like hospital nursing. The year we moved to W———, L——— was away the whole day and went on long business trips. I didn't know anyone, couldn't go anywhere, I didn't care about the house and couldn't catch up with the work. I then got to know a woman with three children who stayed at home while her husband went back to school to get his second Ph.D.; she brought me Friedan's *Feminine Mystique*. That was the beginning.

One woman described it this way:

> I've been hit by Women's Lib. I have less of a tendency to take a back seat. I'm more conscious that what we do suits him; we

never go on vacations. Once J———went to Hawaii. It was a last-minute decision to travel and he came back from work to have me do his laundry. I'll never forgive him for it. Things are better now, more equal. Society backs women up now.

What are the effects of the change in consciousness? The wife of one of the doctors expressed it this way: 'Women's Lib is bad. . . . It makes you question. You feel you're unworthy. What am I doing? Am I his slave?' The most important effect is the feeling of the wife that she has a right to talk about what is bothering her. Nine of the ten women (the wife of the pension consultant was the exception) felt they were making legitimate demands on their husbands. Whether the women think that the husbands agree to the legitimacy of their demands is another question.

E——— said he agreed with me but he really didn't – until recently.

When I speak about my problems, he doesn't answer or says there are no problems. I don't know whether he really doesn't see it or doesn't want to see it.

Did I try to talk about the problems! He doesn't believe that a husband and wife work things out but that this should come naturally.

Most of the wives felt that the conflict over their mutual roles led to changes in their relationships. The four women who returned to work or school felt that the Women's Movement was crucial for their decision to work outside the household and for their feeling that the demands they were making of their husbands were legitimate. As one woman put it: 'Before I was doing all the work at home. . . . He was busy making it. Now I want my chance.'

Generally, these women who had tried to effect changes in their lives were harassed, angry and depressed. They had married with the expectation of fulfilling the traditional woman's role. As their husbands became busy and absorbed in their professions, they found the role much less satisfying; they were on their own with the children, burdened and bored. According to the women, their first reaction was anger with their husbands but without thinking there was the possibility for actual change. It did not occur to them to work outside the household. After all, their husband's success was important for their possibilities as well. Competition was natural; their husbands had to compete and work hard. As bad as it was, 'that's the way of the world'. It is true they felt their family living was affected by it, their relationship drained because of it, but what could one do? It was only after the impact of the Women's Movement that some of the women felt they could do something about their misery, not by changing society in any way, but as individuals, by leaving their households and participating in a 'more interesting world', as they saw it.

How did the other women deal with being so much on their own? Three reacted by taking over the complete responsibility and decision-making in the household.

I like to do things on my own. If the home became his priority it might not be so good. I like to do things around the house. If I have to watch TV with him, I can't sew.

He has to make decisions even though he has no time to think about them, for example, deciding about the curtains in the house – or he tries to tell me what to do about M——— (their child) – but he's never around so how can he contradict me?

One of the women, who once worked as a secretary very closely with her husband, wanted to return to work. Her husband was against it because he felt it would be improper for someone in her position to be a secretary. How do these women who are unable to return to work because of lack of skill feel about what they are doing?

I'm sometimes bored and depressed. I brood and talk to friends but it doesn't help. Most of them are in the same position – Some have more children, others will go shopping and travel half an hour to get thread.

P——— said at the beginning of the marriage that his work comes first. In his mind, the wife stays at home. Now when I ask questions, he doesn't answer. There's nothing I can do – I'm dependent on him.

It would have been better if I had gone off on my own; he wouldn't have had it all on his shoulders. If I had something to divert myself I wouldn't zero in on the family so much.

I get angry and hysterical; when that happens, he stays at home for a while and when I forget about it again, he goes back to work.

Although these last two women sound as 'down' as the others, I had the feeling from the way they spoke about their husbands that they both had good marriages and an intense relationship with their husbands. They thought their husbands gave as much as they could to them and to their children if one took into account all the work they had to do. It seems that the lack of time, concern with success, competition, do not necessarily cause poor relationships between people even if for most couples they are real strains. In these two families, the wives were very sensitive to their husbands' success-drives as if they were afflictions that had to be reckoned with. Both men were perceived by their wives as being open with them about problems at work and very much enjoying the few hours they did have together.

He is intense, loving and sensitive. I knew that the job was causing it. We were helpless.

Sometimes he comes home after a long day's work and wants to drive up to Boston for the evening. He will never say he won't go out. If it's something I really want to do, he'll be there, no matter what.

For most women involved in consciousness-raising, these redeeming factors would be far from satisfactory. I am, however, trying to look at the marriages from the points of view of the women involved.

For those women who went back to school or work and shared some of the responsibilities with their husbands, there were great time strains. They saw themselves as running to catch up. One woman said there were nights she could not sleep thinking of everything that had to be done and added she was often tense and nervous with the children: 'I sometimes come into the house so exhausted that I can't stand the sound of my children's voices – I feel awful about it and E———has prescribed some tranquillizers for me.' Another woman described the invasion of time pressures into so-called free hours:

> So much doesn't get done. L———does help but it's the quality of the family life. I want more time with the kids, less tension around the house when we are together, less guilt. On Sunday, he spends half the day working and then we have to clean the house or if we don't we know it's not done. So much of the time is programmed there's no time for unplanned fun. This has gone on for so long. I know it's never really going to be reciprocated. . . . I can never have the freedom from responsibility for the children and the house that he has had.

The women described their happiest moments as times when the family was all together, doing things around the house, going to the park, enjoying vacations. Most of the women thought that these occasions together were not frequent enough. Would they have it any other way then? What kind of life would they envision for themselves, especially with regard to work? The women had never thought of any other possibility; they believed their husbands would not be challenged enough by less demanding work. Not only did most of the wives not envision another life for themselves but some mentioned without my asking that they themselves put pressure on their husbands to meet professional and social demands.

> While in residency, he was to write a paper with someone and didn't finish on time. His colleague was critical and so was I – I pressured him to get through.

> When L———was offered a job at a school with more prestige and more money we were both ambivalent. He liked where he was but the other university looked more appealing. I wanted to go back to school and we needed more money. We compromised ourselves – because a better university wanted him, we went there. We couldn't turn it down because of the money and prestige reasons.

One woman whose husband worked perhaps the longest hours of anyone in the group said she would not mind if he took a position with even greater responsibility. 'It couldn't be worse than this and I don't believe it will get better anyway.'

The sense of the future was more specific for the women who had decided to work or to go back to school. They looked forward to their children growing up and had at least some help from their husbands in the household; they were interested and committed to their work although I do not think that any of them wanted a high-pressured career. They said that they did not want to devote themselves to their work in as single-minded a fashion as their husbands. This feeling seemed general among the ten women interviewed. From a few responses, though, I understood that the women had doubts about whether they could make it in the outside world and a fear of failure. Since they were able to take their status from their husbands' position and that status was important to them, they were reluctant to give up their image of themselves as 'successful wives' for possible failures in other areas. One woman said that her feelings of competition extended to her husband. She thought she could never do anything or involve herself in any area in which her husband was involved because she was very competitive and could never be second best. 'In fact, the other night, he said he wished we could take up something together – photography – but I wasn't at all interested.'

Of the six women who had not begun to study or work, two wanted very much to go back to school or work but were unsure of how exactly to go about it. Three said they were happy staying at home although one of the three thought vaguely of opening a greenhouse one day. The remaining woman who was bored and depressed at home and yet who was discouraged by her husband when she wanted to take a secretarial job, hoped that the new house they were building in the country would entice him to stay home from work a bit more and give them something to do together.

Effects of tensions on family relations; the male professionals' perspective

Several, although certainly not all, of the men I spoke with shared with me some very serious problems in their personal lives. Two of the men had been seriously ill in recent years. Another indicated some physical problem as the reason he exercised every day and two others said they had intense psychological disturbances. I cannot say that these problems were directly caused by the work experience but pressures such as heavy work loads and the tenseness about success seemed definitely related to their difficulties.

I had good marks and came out second in my class of three hundred. I was glad I did. My ego would have been hurt if it hadn't gone that way. I had scholarships and assistantships and then my problem started. It got worse and worse so that I couldn't stand in front of a class anymore.

Two years ago, I was pushing hard. I developed a severe back problem but didn't have time to take care of it. My wife hauled me to lectures. I had such terrific pain. If I had taken my time it would have never come to this. While recovering, I got ill with a virus; I had only a fifty per cent chance of recovering. One night, I got a very high fever; the doctors couldn't control it. . . .

1973 was my worst year. I was passed over and didn't become the manager. . . . I was severely depressed.

The heavy work loads, the tensions about success, the feelings shared by nearly all the men about never being able to sit back and take it easy, led many to put all their emotional energy into their work. The emotional investment into other areas of their lives, especially for the older men, was so small compared to what they put into work that they really had no other place to turn to, to give them what they thought they were getting from their professional life.

As I look back, I regret not spending enough time with the kids but that's water over the dam. Other men went on trips with their wives. I couldn't get that priority high enough. I was selfish. I didn't take time off. I wasn't interested in anything else . . . I like to work. It's more satisfying than other things. I haven't given anything else a chance.

Often, as in the case of at least three men I spoke with, it appeared that never-ending pressures leave the men without self-confidence, without a feeling of self-worth, so that every additional invitation for work is an indication that the professional is still acceptable. The professionals I spoke with felt reluctant to turn down requests to serve on committees, opportunities to contribute to professional journals and offers of increased responsibility. Any setback makes the professional feel less of a human being, any accomplishment at work assures him, at least temporarily, he is successful. Once these feelings become associated with difficult political and social factors, such as cliques in the departments with competing demands or difficulties relating to colleagues, rather than the nature of the task at hand, the reactions are more complicated and involve personal areas he cannot always touch or deal with rationally.

> For a long time, I looked for another doctor to work with. I found one who only stayed a few months, however. He didn't intend to stay and I had looked for him for so long. It's like marrying the wrong person. I lost confidence about my ability to see into people. It's ego damaging. I have to begin another search.

The academic who had experienced rejection in his department, despite his excellent academic background, reacted by moving to a far less prestigious college where he had a lower salary, no assistants, no colleagues in his field and no supportive courses in other departments.

A few people try intellectually to understand their professional experiences; others are too busy trying to 'make it' to reflect on what is happening to them. How is it possible for them, under such circumstances, to respect themselves and to really care for others?

At the beginning of their careers, there was intense strain for which both husbands and wives were unprepared:

> When I had to sleep in the hospital, my wife became irritable. When I came home and wanted to relax with the paper, she got angry. She wanted someone to talk to. I couldn't blame her.

> I would help the kids with homework until ten or eleven and then go back to the hospital. I was tired and irritable. We had hassles – my wife got angry. At the beginning of my career, the kids would sulk when I left. We'd irritate each other.

> When I first started my work I bitched and moaned. My wife didn't like to hear it; she got up-tight and aggravated.

The academic who reacted with 'isolation and anxiety' when his first years in a new department were unsuccessful found his family life strongly affected. 'I was putting in a lot of hours and sat around silently. It wasn't much fun. My wife was also isolated – no one wanted to see her so we had even more tension. . . . We argued about my being away so much.'

In my interviews with wives of professionals, two of the younger women fully expected that when their husbands were established, their schedules would be easier and they would be able to share more of their lives together. A few of the men I spoke with also had such hopes. One lawyer and a psychiatrist in private practice actually spent a great deal of time with their families. Most of the men, however, continued to leave their families for time left over from work.

My family is always competing for time. It's a way of life. My wife has never known anything else. (Doctor)

I had no time for my family . . . I sacrificed personal goals. . . . We don't play games like I'm doing it for the good of the family. I do this work because I enjoy it. My wife tries not to focus her life on mine, to be dependent on me, on my free time. I don't want her to watch the door at five. . . . Most of my research work I do at home now. Our biggest source of tension was when I went to the laboratory six nights of the week. She realized, though, I had to do my work. You're not good company if you want to be somewhere else. A lot of women wouldn't put up with it. (Natural scientist)

The women who don't accept the doctor's time schedule don't stay married. (Doctor)

My wife has come to accept it. We had problems until she did. I do work at odd hours or odd times – actually, twenty-four hours a day. Three years ago, I was working on a project in——. The pressures are severe to meet deadlines. I sacrificed the time with my family. My wife said I was detached. I argued and withdrew. She said I was incommunicative and not interested in the kids. . . . The kids are growing up and they need me the most. (Engineer)

Several of the men I spoke with found it difficult to focus on their wives' problems, on what their wives were really experiencing. Their comments on what the wives did all day usually described their volunteer work and other out-of-the-house activities. Just as they defined themselves in terms of the work they were doing, their comments on their wives' lives focused on how the women were 'making it' in the community. They kept returning to the discussion of their work. The engineer finally complained: 'I'm surprised you're asking me these questions. I thought you were going to ask me about my work.' How did the men see their wives coping with the heavy work demands of their husbands? A few were quite happy not to think of these problems at all. Most of the men recognized that their wives spent long periods of time alone with the children, that most were irritable and strained when their husbands were away for long periods of time, but the men thought they got used to it, accepted it. It was only when their wives became visibly upset that they tried, at least for a time, to share more in the family.

> When I see my wife is getting tense, I watch out and try to avoid it. If an event is important to her, I try to be there. Sometimes, I don't realize she wants to do something. Last week, she mentioned something casually about apple-picking. When the day came, she had her heart set on it. I told her to go ahead, that I had work to do. Then she got upset, so I went along. (Natural scientist)

In this particular case, the husband does a great deal of research at home; this new schedule has been a great relief to his wife, who used to spend many days and evenings alone. I will come back to the reasons for his change.

> I use my wife as a sounding board. She gives me advice. She says I don't give her enough time. We can't both talk at once. Fortunately, her parents are here.

> My wife doesn't like it if I work too much. I come home in a great mood; my wife's in a terrible mood because she's with the kids and she's exhausted. I feed on depression – she does that, too.

> When I was coming up in the organization, I was out three or four nights a week. It didn't bother my wife, . . . We had our children.

However, later on in our talk, this last man said that with the birth of the last child, his wife had a 'mild nervous breakdown'. 'She wanted my sympathy and help. For a while I took more time. . . . I helped her with some of her daily activities, along with our older daughter.'

In two of the families, the wives were outgoing and lively, encouraging the social participation of their husbands; with time, however, that changed; the women became more withdrawn and the husbands more social and outgoing.

> During the first two or three years of work, I was very depressed and came home depressed. She didn't know what to do. . . . In a way, now she misses my not being depressed because she's not needed that much. . . . At first, she pushed me to get out. Now at a party, when I feel in control, I'm fine and she's uptight.

> My wife is helpful, attractive. She helped me with my shyness, my unwillingness to be aggressive socially. Now she's the opposite, she's not that way any more. . . . She's less aggressive socially and I am more so. I developed self-confidence in a way that I hadn't before.

The carrying over of one's professional position into one's social life is not surprising in a society that puts such a high value on occupational achievement.

The men sometimes get mixed messages from their wives. On the one hand, they are asked to spend more time at home; on the other hand, a few of the wives are quite ambitious for their husbands. I found the same contradiction in my interviews with women who did not work outside the home.

> My wife felt I never had enough time for her, to listen to her. Now there's too much togetherness. She wonders whether I'm working hard enough.

> She wanted to see me with a prestigious post connected with———I didn't feel it was important. But at her insistence and her family's, I made an approach to———.

> My wife worked on me to push my advisor.

> My wife thinks I should be higher.

In most families, however, the wives want their husbands to be at home more. Some may not realize that their ambitions for their husbands' careers are time-consuming. Most husbands, too, are concerned about their absence; they particularly try to spend time with their children and have guilt feelings if they are not able to.

Once my family joined me out west at a conference. I left to attend a lecture at another university several hundred miles away. The lecture was terrible. My family was having a great time. I missed a great family experience and really regretted it. (Natural scientist)

I did more work than I should have . . . I should have given more hours to the family. We're a close unit. If I had sons it would have been tragic. I wouldn't have had enough time to give to my sons. The girl's model is her mother. My father was always away. My mother was competent – aggressive for us. My wife is the same. . . . On————, I was the only father coming to school. (Doctor)

Even in the marriages where the husbands were nearly totally occupied by their work there was still some contact between the husbands and wives. Aside from reading, watching television, doing sports together and occasionally attending concerts and the theatre, a lot of conversation revolved around the husband's problems at work. In two instances, the professionals made definite changes in their lives; these changes came about because they were ill but, I had the impression, had long-term effects on how they saw their future development. They did not reduce their ambitions very much but they seemed to be making a strong effort to balance their interests and concerns.

One of the older men went for a walk with me and said that we (the younger guys) were doing well and that we should calm down. Hearing him say it helped. . . . When I told the doctor my schedule he said I was insane. I told him everyone else worked that hard and he said it wasn't normal. I realized that one person wasn't all that important. If I did die, life would just go on. Now I do sports – hiking, camping, running, swimming.

I've had back problems for several months now. Before that, I worked a seventy-hour week at least. . . . My condition is most fortunate. I learned I could take the summer off. One always wants to feel needed. I felt I couldn't go away. I could have enjoyed all those summers. . . . This summer I was able to read; it was my first novel in ten years. We had more to talk about.

Three of the men, the lawyer, the psychiatrist in private practice and the professor in the natural sciences, seemed especially committed to their marriages; one was among the busiest professionals I spoke to. I am not able completely to understand why their marriages seemed more successful than the others but they all took for granted that their wives, their families were a tremendously important part of their lives; all three came from a somewhat traditional family culture. One was brought up in Rhode Island and remained there, part of a large Jewish family; the second was brought up in a Catholic family and the third was Protestant and attended religious services regularly. All three had wives who accepted more traditional role divisions within the family, even with tentative plans to return to work later on. All three husbands had a great deal of respect for what their wives were doing. Two of the men, the lawyer and the psychiatrist in private practice, were less ambitious and less pressured at work; they spent considerable time with their families. The professor in the natural sciences thought they were better off than a lot of families they know even though he felt busy and pressured at work.

We can handle separation, we have confidence in our relationship. . . . We never set time limits on how long I can be away like other couples who say no more than two weeks. My wife doesn't feel burdened with the kids or resentful. We're not like that; my wife doesn't feel put upon. She went away for five weeks when her dad was ill. I took everything over with my son but I didn't feel put upon.

It is not that his wife simply accepted his absences from home; those years he spent so many evenings at the laboratory were very difficult for her and caused great tension in the family, according to her husband. During a recent trip across the United States, she was angry when he dropped her off at relatives for two days and went to a motel to work. 'She threatened to go to the Cape alone for the weekend. I don't think she will but she can if she wants to.' Again, although these conditions seem bleak at times, the people involved view them in a context of a stable and loving marital relationship; at least, it seemed this way to me after our talk. . . .I did not speak with his wife.

The lawyer said he was perfectly content to spend long periods of time at home. Every weekend in winter, he went with his wife and children to their country house to ski. He did not work the long hours the other professionals did; he seemed less pressured than they were. He made the following comments on his wife's role in the household:

> I'm not remote but my wife does the housework. . . . She observes the children and has more contact with them. She's a woman and a mother. No one does that better. That role is deprecated here. We don't though. She feels motherhood is an acceptable role and is not discontented. Friedan wouldn't be happy with her.

The psychiatrist in private practice seemed to have made a personal commitment to his family based not only on his Catholic background but on his professional observations.

> I do a lot of things for my wife that are really for me. For example, if I take her out for dinner, I go out. If I bring her flowers, I enjoy them, too. . . . I believe that nothing is more important than the family. I let nothing interfere with it. I had patients who fulfilled all their dreams and were successful. Now they have nothing – no friends, maybe not even each other.

I assumed that men absorbed in their work lives would have some sympathy for the work ambitions of their wives; at the same time, they are able to give so much to their own profession only because everything at home is taken care of for them. How would they feel if they could no longer take that for granted?

Eight of the ten wives worked outside the household after they were married (see Table 2.2 p. 24). One of the women who had completed her law degree was not able to take a job because they left the country immediately after completing their graduate studies. Several expressed an interest in returning to work. The woman who had neither completed college nor worked outside the house after marrying thought of starting a business; she was uncertain, however, of whether someone 'in her position' should do so.

The two women who, according to their husbands, did not express any desire to work outside the household were the wife of the lawyer and the wife of one of the doctors I spoke with. The lawyer spent, perhaps of all the professionals, the most time with his family. The doctor's wife spent several years working after their marriage and felt perfectly content to stay at home. Of course, I did not speak with her; her husband was one of the busiest professionals I spoke with and she was one of the wives 'who never knew anything else . . . and was used to it'.

Many women did extensive volunteer work in their communities. A few took courses. The husbands all approved of these involvements outside the house.

I want her to be involved. People are happier when they are involved. She took some classes and I encouraged that. Right now, her goal is to straighten out the house after our travelling. (Natural scientist)

Since I've gone into practice, she became a volunteer. She has skills . . . she was president of the women's association at the hospital. I'm agreeable to that – my mother did that, too. (Doctor)

According to their husbands, most of the women did not think of a career outside the household when they first married and had children. 'When we first met she wanted to be a wife.' (Psychiatrist) Women who had made traditional marriages, then, were now considering a return to work. Since I did not speak with them, I can only guess at their reasons based on my interviews with women who stayed at home.

The reactions of the men were as many-sided as the reactions of the wives to the ambitions of their husbands.[3] Many men with young children are hesistant about their wives working outside the home because they fear the children will not be cared for properly (see also Holmstrom, 1972, p.142), because they are afraid they will have to take on an increased burden themselves and because there is the possibility that the relationship they have to each other would be affected.

Women with masculine identities and men with feminine identities have problems. If a woman decides to be boss and works like a man, she doesn't give him enough space. . . . Motherhood is full-time work. I need the family. Most men's jobs are dull. My wife can do anything she wants, go out with the girls – have tea – I don't have time for that. Someone has to stay at home with the children. It can be the man but women seem to do it better. . . . It would change our lives if my wife went back. It would depend on the time. I wouldn't permit her to while the children were young. Her job is to spend time with the kids. Nothing is more important – and she agrees. Later on, she can go back. (Psychiatrist)

At the same time, some of these men knew that it was not easy for the wives to have so much responsibility for the care of the children. 'She never felt one hundred per cent a mother and can't understand those mothers who do. She is forced in twenty-four hours a day. . . . She lives in the future. . . . It would be great *when*. She doesn't feel needed.' (Scientist)

No one mentioned the Women's Movement unless specifically asked and then the typical answer was that their wives were not affected by it, did not identify with those women and did not feel pressured by them in any way.

As the men advance in their careers and the children are in high school and college, they seem more prepared to have their wives work. Firstly, by that time, there is usually hired help in the household and not so much to do physically for the care of the children. Secondly, the men realize that their wives are not happy spending long hours alone at home, shopping or even in volunteer work and they, for the most part, are either unable or unwilling to spend more time with them.

My wife took courses and is certified as an elementary school teacher and an art teacher for students with learning disabilities. She still can't get a job. Our relationship would improve if she worked. If she's at home, she's dependent and doesn't do her own thing. That explains the differences in our approaches. She's too involved with all of us. (Engineer)

It would improve our relationship and give her self-confidence, something practical to do. It would get her mind off worries and other things. She's a worrier. (President – large organization)

A few of the professionals thought that a higher income would improve their relationship. In the case of one academic, having his wife stay at home was a financial burden; astonishingly enough, two other men who suggested this advantage of the wife's working had very high incomes and huge homes. Most of the women now consider working outside the home. The husbands seem quite agreeable when the children are older. Several patterns, however, have already been firmly established. The first is that the husband's professional work is of top priority. The wife takes over the household so that he may concentrate on his development in his career; he does some work in the household but she has most of the responsibility. After the children are well taken care of and his wife's dependence on him becomes a bit uncomfortable, he thinks it might be a good idea for her to work outside the home. By that time, however, she has difficulty getting back into her field. In addition, if he has devoted all his energy and attention to his work, there may be little to fall back on in their personal relationship to each other. He is left with his work, she with a few women friends and hopefully some relationship to the children. In a few instances, the husband and wife had a stable and caring relationship that would probably continue whether or not the wife was able to find work outside the home.

The effects of work pressures and tensions on friendships

It was not astonishing to discover that, in contrast to their wives, most of the men had no close friends. The two professionals who said they knew men with whom they could really talk were the psychiatrist in private practice and the busy, but family-committed academic. A few were able to share with relatives but most men were no longer living in an area where they had either old friends or relatives.

I am, of course, not suggesting that these men have no social life. Often, however, social life revolves around the demands of work. As indicated before, it may be useful for advancing in an organization. During the years one professional was moving up in his organization, the president invited him to come with his wife to visit him for the weekend:

We would be invited along with several other couples to his

place in ———. Even after we argued like hell about something, we'd be invited. I was anti-social but he got me out of it and made me an extrovert. I wasn't completely comfortable. I kept thinking about the work but we always met interesting people there.

Only one of the men said that his colleagues were his good friends. They socialized together and knew each other's children; however, he would not speak to them about really personal problems. Two of the men, the psychiatrist in the hospital and the lawyer, did very little socializing with colleagues. The psychiatrist listed a number of characteristics his friends should have, which included being upper middle class or rich. A few of the men tried to understand the nature of the 'friendship' they have with their colleagues:

My friends are nice but they're very competitive. They're image conscious and concerned with how other people see them. They build a house that has to be just so. One of the wives works as a nurse just so they can get all those things. (Scientist)

There are two couples we are close to in New York; our closest friends are also people we spend the summer with. . . . We find them outside of Boston. Here, we live in a ghetto. There is no generosity; there is competition for material things, for example, driving a Mercedes. . . . Here we really have acquaintances. (Doctor)

Are friendships of real value as ends in themselves? The last professional quoted who found it difficult to have friendships where he lived and worked, on the one hand expressed the desire to make friends perhaps among people in other fields and on the other hand had neither the time nor the commitment to add real friendship to his life.

When I come home I don't want to find people here. I give everything at work; I have no more to give. I want to be with my family and hear their problems – and not too many . . . . Familiarity breeds contempt. You're afraid to tell anyone anything because they might advertise it. True friends are not a realistic goal here. There's too much togetherness. You get too involved with close friends. You never escape.

This man I think articulated the feelings of some of the other men I spoke with. How close is it possible to be with men you are competing with? How much can you reveal of yourself to them? Are your old ideals of friends as ends in themselves compatible with friendship with someone you may hurt or leave behind in order to advance yourself? Is an advantage for one a disadvantage for the other? Can you afford to spend time with people who do not help you advance professionally? These problems are magnified for male professionals because their very upbringing discouraged their revealing emotions to other people. From my observations, I also noticed that some men find it difficult not to compete in any situation in which they find themselves with other male professionals, the most likely group they would associate with – an inclination which clearly does not encourage the growth of friendships. As up-and-coming busy professionals they may not be as intensely aware of their lack of real friendships; they are certainly active enough socially. As they got older, however, they become aware that 'for some reason' they do not seem to have any real friends. 'I don't have close friends. It bothers me. Perhaps I could talk to an old childhood friend of mine. It bothers my wife, too, because she does have friends.' In a few instances, where there was not great pressure to socialize with colleagues, the wife made the social arrangements with the women she was friendly with. Unfortunately, the man was not always able to share interests and values with the husbands of his wives' friends.

Conclusion

The effects of work pressures and competition are far-reaching. A few of the men made a connection between their lives at work and their mental and physical difficulties. Several had invested so much attention and energy in their work that they were unable to get much satisfaction from other areas of their lives. Although their first years in the profession were the most difficult, they continued to take on extremely heavy work loads. Part of their continual work commitment seemed to be related to the habit of work, which for some of the men had been encouraged even while they were very young; their devotion to their work was also a public indication of professional commitment. A few of the men had doubts about how good they were; these doubts were related to professional achievement. Even after working as professionals for several years, many were not confident of their successful behaviour in the organization. Inside the place of work, colleagues were sometimes viewed as potential competitors. Outside work, the professionals' way of looking at people and what people worked at coloured even their most intimate relationships. Karen Horney (1937, pp. 284–6) discusses the relationship between pressures and ambitions at work and personal relationships in capitalist society. She sees competitive behaviour, even the early competitive behaviour in the family, as a response to culturally conditioned stimuli rather than as a general human phenomenon.

A few of the men were very concerned and caring about their family lives but many found it difficult to focus on what their wives were really experiencing. Their comments on what the wives did all day usually described their out-of-the-house activities, how the women were 'making it' in the community. They recognized that their wives spent long periods of time alone with the children, that most were irritable and strained when their husbands were away for long periods of time but the men thought they got used to it, accepted it.

Most of the women saw their husbands' will and effort to succeed as a burden for their personal lives together; yet at the same time, they encouraged their husbands' ambitions and enjoyed the rewards of success. Few understood the ambitions of their husbands as related to the inducements and pressures exerted by educational and work institutions. Rather, they saw these coming from natural competitive drives or family upbringing. In the end, they thought, the individual decides how he is going to live and is responsible for his ambitions, his strivings, his life outside work. Theory and past empirical studies suggest, however, that arrangements at work have a strong, though partial, influence on the life patterns of men and women, and my subsequent interviews confirm this expectation. Clinging to beliefs in the importance of personality and rejecting explanations based on social and economic structure is indicative of the social-psychological nature of much of our common sense. It may serve to protect a belief in individuality in a world of social pressures and reflects the difficulties in understanding the working of complex industrial societies.

With security and recognition, both husbands and wives seemed to be feeling intense relief, and for the husbands there was an increasing ability to widen their emotional attention. However, the women continued to be both depressed and 'unfulfilled'.

What did the women want from their husbands? The women who just returned to school or work needed concrete help from their husbands, cleaning the house, taking care of the children, etc. All women, however, desired a greater involvement of their husbands in the life of the family and I am inclined to interpret many concrete wishes and demands as a desire for evidence of commitment for their shared life.

It seems that until women pushed hard, their husbands often did not listen to them and, furthermore, that there were several men who did not respond to the demands of their wives even then. At least half of the women felt their husbands were not concerned with the world in which the women lived. These women thought their husbands were insensitive to their emotional needs. This is evident from their complaints of unsuccessful efforts to talk to them about their problems at home and in their married life, from the anger expressed toward their husbands, from their occasional hysteria. They felt powerless to affect their own situation and thought any solution coming from their husbands unlikely.

Some of the women who had earlier expected to follow traditional wifely roles now thought of working outside the home. The men felt more open to this possibility when the children were older. Not only would they then have less of a burden in the household to share, but their wives would be less dependent on them, thereby allowing them to concentrate their energies on work.

In trying to understand the effects of work pressures on family relationships, it is important to understand that the same marriage may have many different and often contradictory aspects. Even if it seemed in my talks that the couples were taking some shape and form, there were other tendencies as well, contradicting what I was seeing and concluding. In the same relationship, when I thought I saw neglect and abandonment, there was care and concern; when I thought there was acceptance, I also felt anger; when I sensed there was communication, I also saw isolation.

Most of the men had no close friends they could talk to really personally. Their time and energy were committed to their work lives. Friendships with colleagues were restricted; they often socialized together but they expected no more than the usual comradeship among colleagues from each other. As some of the men got older, they realized they had no deep relationships with anyone but their wives, and not always with them. Both men and women experienced considerable frustrations and tensions which derived from the husband's work life. Yet neither husband nor wife seemed to question the legitimacy of the system; men who had difficulty at work and were treated unfairly felt they should have somehow been better; women whose husbands worked extremely long hours had great ambition for them – their success was somehow a fair exchange.

Appendix:

Notes on interviewing
I decided to use a rather structured interview guide despite an anticipated degree of unnaturalness of conversation, because of my fear of talking too generally and not getting to enough specifics. With the 'at home' wives, I started with rather formal questions about the husband's work. It may be argued that asking the wife to describe her husband's work in detail might have set up a certain sympathetic understanding in her mind. Perhaps, it would have been better to start with some general questions about the wife's emotional state and see her initial reactions. However, I feared such a beginning might scare her and that more formal information-seeking questions would be a more relaxing way to begin.

As a reaction to the tendency of interviewers to feed answers to respondents, I tried to be careful with my phrasing and decided that if the respondent did not include my particular concerns, then to probe. The probing is also a problem. If I do not get tensions mentioned and then ask about them, I will discover more tensions related to the husband's job than if I did not mention them at all. For example, competitiveness at work was an area in which I felt concerned about injecting my suspected answer into the question; again, if I probed here I always probed with the possibility that the respondent's husband did not see himself in a particularly competitive situation or even if he did, it might not be causing him any particular tensions.

A few of the women I selected to interview were women I knew rather well. The particular advantages of deciding to include a few friends were the possibility of 'hanging around the house' a bit more, the larger perspective I had on the family and the relationship they were describing, and the honesty and effort I expected the women to make to try to be as truthful to what they were feeling as possible. The disadvantages were that they were people I saw often; therefore, they might have been more guarded in revealing really intense problems in the relationship, really strong emotional hang-ups that might change my basic perceptions of them. I do not mean that no problems were discussed but when a respondent suggested that 'our emotional relationship causes many problems' outside the work situation and I then asked the respondent if she could be more specific and received a second vague answer, I was afraid of probing and taking advantage of our friendship, of calling on the friendship for getting information rather than respecting the privacy of the respondent. Thus, I did not ask all the questions I wanted to. With a stranger that I had never seen before and would probably never see again, there might be a problem of trusting me to keep the information strictly confidential. However, the respondent could also have been more open and I might have pushed her harder. One woman with whom I was not well acquainted was most controlled. Although she did admit to problems, and very serious ones, I felt that what she was saying was not what I sensed was happening. One does not only influence a respondent by the very questions one asks but I was responding (and thus influencing her response) to something about my perception of her – her control, the unwillingness to abandon herself in a reflective sense to the intensity of her emotional deprivation, at least in the conversation itself. I then reverted to a more formal style of interviewing although I again and again had the feeling of wanting to throw the questions away, to deviate much further from my pre-arranged questions than one does in probing and to allow her to structure the course of our conversation according to her needs. This brings me back to the problem of the interview guide itself. Except with total strangers and probably not even then, a problem in using a structured interview for such personal questions is that a questionnaire is an unusual way of getting at such information.

Friendship and conversation in friendship include an exchange of confidences. If one does all the confiding in a situation where the point is not to seek out sympathy or help from a friend in solving a problem, but to respond to questions, the exchange is not a balanced one.

I decided therefore to occasionally make some personal comment that indicated, for example, some influence on my life, but at the same time I was most concerned about that comment not pushing the respondent in any direction. I think such exchanges helped the openness of the talks.

Some of the professional men hesitated to speak with me because they did not want to use up valuable time. 'This may be important to you but it means nothing to me. I don't have time to sit chatting; I have a department and other responsibilities.' This particular professional spent twenty minutes on the telephone telling me of his schedule, his guests and his travels before he allowed me to phone his secretary and arrange the interview.

Thankfully, I did not have such difficulties with all the male respondents. Once we were together all of them were polite and tried to be cooperative. Because many did have difficulties being open emotionally, however, I thought at first they were deliberately not sharing with me. After one difficult interview, I expressed this feeling to a man who had been elegantly polite but distant. I told him I did not mean to criticize him but I felt that he did not share a great deal with me; perhaps I was not specific enough or I did not push him enough. . . . He seemed very surprised and answered that he had told me more than he had ever told anyone.

Later on, I thought that either the men did not reflect about these issues or they were so defensive that the problems they were willing to talk about seemed superficial to me. They found it extremely difficult to talk about their early childhood and even their early experiences in school. They found it difficult to focus on the feelings of their wives and what their lives at home were like. One man kept returning to his work; another was surprised that I was 'asking such questions'. The interviews with American professional men were certainly the most difficult interviews I have done.

I tried to deal with this lack of openness in my interviews in two ways, first by accepting what I was hearing and second, by being as compassionate as I could be while listening to what they felt able to share with me about themselves. My trying to understand, rather than to be dissatisfied, resulted in several very good interviews. Some of the men said it was an important talk for them, a talk which gave them a chance to reflect on a wide variety of issues that they usually did not think much about. Such acceptance of the men I spoke with had strange consequences for my analysis. When I took apart what they said, I had strong feelings that most were overinvolved in their work and under-developed in other areas. Many of their reactions made me angry. Yet I continue to have the feeling that I am unfair to them, that they cannot control their responses, that they would care if only they could, a reaction that fits well into my view of how important social institutions are in shaping the most intimate responses of people.

In contrast to at least a few of the women I spoke to, I had no close friends among these men. Their names were given to me by colleagues I knew in their fields. They, therefore, did not feel as obligated as some of the women to question themselves intensely. However, I had a better feeling not using the friendship for my sociological interests. At times, I also felt freer pressing a question with them than with women I would be in contact with again.

If the interview took place at home, which was the case for half of the men I spoke with, I tried to talk afterwards with both the husbands and wives together. I was relieved that two of the husbands, at least, were more able to focus on aspects of their relationship when their wives were around. I also got some sense of how the wives felt about the issues I was interested in, some groans when their husbands proposed to do even more work, some sharing of their isolation. After one professional said he did not want to come home after a busy day and find visi-tors, his wife added, 'but I'm all pent up wanting to talk to people'. Not surprisingly then, I had a bit more of a feeling of the two together when I could actually spend some time talking to them.

Finally, I could not help believing that the men, with all their problems, were still better off than the wives I spoke with who were more isolated than they were and who felt more neglected than they did. The husbands had an intense interest in their work, the wives in a relationship that was often more noticeable in its absence. The children and even close friends, it seems, were not able to make up for that loss.

Interview guide
This outline of questions was used in the interviews with 'at-home' women. Appropriate variations guided my interviews with all other groups.

1. Description of family.
2. What exactly is your husband doing?
3. When did he start doing this work?
4. How does the normal work-day (-week) look in the life of your husband?
   travel
   moves from one office to next,
   hours at work,
   brings work home.
5. How are decisions at his place of work made? Does your husband make decisions that affect the work life of other people (that may cause dissatisfaction and friction)?
6. Is there somebody he is responsible to? What decisions does that person make for him (and how do these decisions affect the husband's life in the present and in the future)?
7. If things worked out ideally, what would be the professional development of your husband? (check for open-endedness of aspiration. Is there a definite point of having made it?) Is there a lot competition for position he looks for – or wanted? Is providing for old age a problem? Is the husband concerned about it?
8. How do his colleagues get along with him? Are the relations occasionally tense? (Where tensions come from, how frequent – competition between colleagues, clique formations?)
9. If husband is solo practitioner: Is bringing in clients, patients, a problem? Has it been? Do you think it will be in the future? Was husband worried about it? Did that problem create extra work and long hours?
10. If partnership: Is bringing in clients, patients a problem? Has it been? Do you think it will be in the future?
    How do the partners compare with each other in respect to bringing in clients?
    Does each keep his own client?
    Does it happen that a client goes from one to another and how is that handled?

Is there competition between (among) partners for bringing in the most clients? If clients are shared, does bringing or not bringing in 'count' with partners?

11. How do you feel about his job in general?
12. Are there special things about your husband's job that cause tensions, problems in the family (husband often away, having enough time for wife and children, absent-minded, calm or tense at home . . . if tense, how does it show when he is at home)?
13. Where do the tensions come from?
14. Did he do something else before? What? (Particular tensions still there? – if not, when did they change?)
15. Can you describe how it was when you first met? What were his ambitions (early tensions)? Did relationship to husband change? How different is it now? Why did that happen? Is there anticipation of it getting better?
16. How would you feel if your husband took a job that would put fewer demands on him but also offered less opportunity for development – gave you a significantly lower income?
17. If you could envision another life for you both, what would it be like, in particular with respect to work?
18. What tensions would still be there?
19. How do you feel about what you are doing?
20. When you first had children, what did you and your husband think you would be doing (staying at home, going to work, both)?
21. Do you see your situation changing? When? What would make this change possible (relief from children, increase of husband's responsibility in household)?
22. Now, this is very difficult to do, but still is it possible to say whether your husband gives priority to work or to his role in the family? Suppose he had to make a choice, putting less energy into one or the other? How do you feel about it?
23. Do people have a choice about all this or is the priority for work set by the society?
24. Suppose your husband were to lower his ambitions in his present work. How could he do it? What are the problems (reactions of colleagues, sanctions against his lack of commitment)?
25. What are some of the situations in which you are happiest? (Frequent?)

26. Do you have time to talk to your closest friends about what is bothering you? Does your husband talk to friends about things that bother him?
27. Could you tell me the last year you finished in school? (If not known already, the same information about husband, her parents and his parents – their occupations as well.)
28. Age of respondent.

3 'I am a professional, too'
American dual-career families

Introduction

Loneliness and some of the other problems of the middle-class wife whose main locus of activity is at home are overcome in dual-career marriages. At the same time, there is more work to be done in dual-career families, and new forms of co-operation and of living together have to be found. Interviewing men and women in dual-career families, then, was an important complement to the interviews with men and women in marriages where only the husband worked full-time outside the house. I tried to determine how much the men were willing or able to pursue their professional work and, at the same time, share in family and household tasks so that their wives could also work outside the home. I was interested in how they managed the care of their children and whether they found time and energy for their personal lives together. Furthermore, I wanted to determine the differences between the two kinds of marriages in co-operation, shared interests and personal commitment to work and family life.

Is the dual career family, if consciously and voluntarily chosen, a growing form of middle-class family life that is viable for both the husband and wife? Some social scientists claim that patterns of family life as well as ideas and expectations about it are particularly resistant to change. My interviews with men and women in dual-career families suggest that relationships in these families did not form a whole new way of being in the family. The contrasts with the single-career family were not radical; they remained variations within a common range. The dual-career families represented mixtures of traditional (one-career household) and new family styles, but the new elements – sometimes subtle, sometimes improvised – must not be underestimated. In particular, there was an opening of discussion and a recognition of problems. The concrete effects of both husbands and wives working outside the home forced them to consciously rearrange their lives and to deal practically with the tasks at hand. This was often done with a feeling of shared responsibility for all the issues and chores in the household and family. All of these changes did not, in many cases, produce an ideal work–family life; this seems mostly due to an unchanged institutional environment, to an absence of supportive institutions, such as nursery schools or the provision of main meals at work and school, and to the fact that work roles and work organizations, not particularly well integrated with conventional family roles, are rarely responsive to the problems and needs of people in dual-career families.

I interviewed ten men and ten women and again tried to get a variety of professionals at different stages of their careers and in different forms of employment. In three families, I spoke with both husband and wife, although at separate times. Most of these interviews took place at home or at work and lasted from two to three hours, even longer than the talks I had before. Table 3.1 gives summary information on these respondents. All but one of the respondents had children. Eight of the respondents had spouses in the same profession as their own or very close to it. Nine of the seventeen women[1] about whom I have information had waited several years to return to their professions, in contrast to their husbands. The younger the woman, the more likely she was to continue her profession without a break; that meant also that her work was more likely to be on the same professional level as her husband's.

In two cases, the women have more secure positions than their husbands. The woman psychiatrist is married to an untenured assistant professor; the final tenure decision will be made in two years. The lawyer employed in a private corporation has a more secure position than her husband whose job depends on the results of the next election. In fact, when they moved after law school, she had got the position in the corporation first; then her husband explored his possibilities in the same city.

Family background and the roots of occupational aspiration

As the respondents in earlier interviews, several of the men and women indicated that their parents' demands were important for their own desire to work hard, to go to college, to go to the right college and succeed. Table 3.2 summarizes the educational background and occupation of the respondents' parents. Six of the ten male respondents had experienced upward social mobility; one more had a father who at first had been successful and then failed at what he was doing. Were the upwardly mobile male professionals more ambitious than those with professional parents? The three men who did have professional parents did not appear as overtly ambitious as some of the upwardly mobile men I spoke with. One, for example, did not go to Harvard Medical School where he had been accepted because he was convinced that a Jewish friend had not been admitted to the school because of his religious background. However, it is also true that these men had more opportunities to develop professionally than the other men I spoke with, for example, by having personal connections in the community which were important for their early professional acceptance.

This moderation of ambition due to family advantage was less evident in the women I interviewed although more came from privileged families. Eight of the women had parents who attended college for at least some years and from their parents' backgrounds it was clear that they were far less upwardly mobile than the men. How did their aspirations relate to their family background? Several said they 'always wanted to do something' and 'knew they would always do something', but were not quite sure what they wanted for themselves.

Four women had educated mothers who finished college but never pursued a career; two of their mothers taught before the children were born, another did substitute teaching after their children were in high school. Six mothers had intellectual interests and were active in their communities but never had a formal higher education; all of these mothers, however, had high expectations for their daughters, according to the women I spoke with.

For several of the women it was important not to be dependent on a man, to be self-supporting. In trying to explain why they wanted to be independent financially, even as youngsters, they pointed out that their mothers had experienced difficult marriages or had seen friends divorce and remain alone without financial support.

TABLE 3.1 Summary information on respondents in dual-career families

Profession	Age	Marital history	Occupation of first spouse	Occupation of second spouse	Number of children in family	Number of children at home at present (under age 12 in brackets)
Males						
Lawyer (private practice, employed by government)	32	Previously divorced, at present married	Secretary	Business woman	3	3(3)
Editor	56	First wife died; at present married	Part-time laboratory	Reporter	2	0(0)
Professor and orchestra conductor	60	Married	Musician; teacher	—	4	1(0)
Physician – private practice	50	Married	Graduate student, also working in profession	—	4	4(3)
Assoc. prof. and artist	35	Married	Business	—	2	2(2)
Physicist (private industry)	37	Married	Statistician	—	2	2(2)
Psychiatrist (private practice)	65	Married	High school teacher, administrator	—	2	0(0)

Lawyer – private practice	29	Married	Lawyer		—	0	0(0)
Editor	37	Married	Administrator		—	2	2(1)
Assistant prof.	32	Married	Psychiatrist		—	2	2(2)
Females							
Artist	38	Separated	Prof.; artist		—	2	2(2)
Elem. school teacher	32	Married	Assistant professor		—	2	2(2)
Singer, teacher	45	Previously divorced, at present married	Businessman	Prof.; artist		2	0(0)
Lawyer – private practice	29	Married	Lawyer		—	0	0(0)
Physician – private practice	43	Married	Physician		—	3	2(1)
Assistant professor	39	Married	Professor		—	4	4(2)
Lawyer – private corporation	27	Married	Lawyer		—	1	1(1)
Public administration	47	Married	Professor		—	3	1(0)
Administrator	36	Married	Editor		—	2	2(1)
Psychiatrist – private practice	32	Married	Assistant professor		—	2	2(2)

TABLE 3.2 *Education and occupation of respondents' parents in dual-career families*

Respondent's profession	Education of father	Occupation of father	Education of mother	Occupation of mother
Males				
Lawyer	High school	Machinist	High school	Did not work outside house
Editor	College	Low level management	Professional school	Did not work outside house
Prof.; orchestra conductor	Elementary school	Teacher, carpenter	High school incomplete	Worked in a shop before marriage
Physician	Medical degree	Doctor	College	Did not work outside house
Prof.; artist	College	Owned small business, salesman	High school	Began work in advertising when respondent was in teens because of financial need
Physicist	Elementary school; incomplete	Factory worker	High school incomplete	Clerk
Psychiatrist	High school; profession self-taught	Scientist	High school	Worked in a publishing house before marriage
Lawyer	High school	Subcontractor; real estate	High school	Did not work outside house
Editor	Ph.D.	University professor	College	Part-time research in early years of marriage

Assistant prof.	High school incomplete	Manager of a department in a department store	High school	Secretary – began after children finished school
Females				
Artist	College	Pilot	College	Did not work outside house
Elem. school teacher	College – incomplete	Photographer	College	Elem. school teacher – before children were born
Singer and teacher	College	Engineer	College	Laboratory assistant
Lawyer – private practice	Elem. school; afterwards, private tutor	Businessman	College – incomplete	Worked as saleswoman after daughter was in college
Physician – private practice	College	Accountant	High school	Secretary before marriage
Assistant prof.	College – incomplete	Banker	College – incomplete	Did not work outside house
Lawyer – private corporation	College	Manufacturer	College – incomplete	Did not work outside house
Public administration	Elementary school	Manager of a farm	Elementary school	Did not work outside house
Administration	College	Businessman	College	Did substitute high school teaching after children were in high school
Psychiatrist	Ph.D.	College professor	College	Elementary school teacher before children were born

> My mother was strong and dominating. She had known women who were left without support. . . . She told me it was important to have something to do, that it was important not to be dependent. (Female lawyer)

> My mother and father divorced and she had no support. She was helpless. I decided never to be helpless. (Female artist)

That these women were ambitious no matter what their socioeconomic background is not surprising. They could not have easily achieved their professional goals otherwise. But their aspirations were not simply rooted in necessity. They were nourished by the encouragement from parents and especially their mothers. In addition to the desire for independence, several women reported that their mothers felt that they had not developed themselves as much as they would have liked. (See the similar findings of Rapoport and Rapoport, 1976, and Hoffman and Nye, 1974.) These mothers impressed on their daughters the importance of fulfilling their potential.

Furthermore, as was already shown in the talks with women who began part-time work or resumed their studies after staying at home with the children, the Women's Movement played an important role by giving nearly all of them a sense of legitimacy for their professional goals; for the older women it was a source of support years after they had made the decision to return to professional life without such backing. Finally, for younger women especially, work organizations were becoming more open to hiring women and so there were increased possibilities for them to practise their professions.

The school experiences of men and women in dual-career families

The impressions and memories of early school experiences revolved around many of the same feelings expressed in the single-career families – competition, tension, shame, submission, boredom and fear of failure. For the men disappointments were related to both failure in class and in sports.

> I was disappointed our basketball team didn't make the league, that I couldn't make the first team in football. I was a three

letter man, though, track, basketball and football. However, it's one thing to be on the team; it's something else to be a star. I wanted to be an all-American athlete. (Male lawyer)

Several men mentioned their training and participation in sports as helpful preparation for achieving generally.

> The competition in sports helped mould people in an aggressive, win way although not cut-throat. You develop pride in doing better than other people. Boys play from the third or fourth grade. I always wanted to win; I never liked losing. . . . All this, I see as positive. (Male lawyer)

Not all the respondents, however, reacted well to the competition they experienced in school. Women seemed to have greater difficulty in dealing with the competition than men. 'Every time there was a spelling contest, I threw up. I think it's the tension that brought it on. That was my worst schooling experience.' (Female lawyer) Although these women were able to graduate successfully from professional school, several had difficulties.

> Law school definitely affected my life. They used the Socratic method, calling and drilling you for an entire period. Once a professor drilled a student for two hours in a row. The experiences were intimidating, and I became more nervous. That continues now. (Female lawyer)

Not only was there academic competition, but several of the respondents were sensitive to social competition and class differences in the school. 'I had problems because the girls were conscious of class. That was also true of the private school I went to later on. I was glad to get into public school for my last two years.' (Female singer) One male professional, although coming from a professional family, was brought up in the country. His entrance into a prestigious private school brought him into contact with city children and a different life style.

> I felt out of place, socially inadequate. I didn't date, I lived in the country. I was associating with people who weren't my people. I didn't like their city manners and their dress. Now they are my natural associates; then I despised them. I was at

the bottom of the heap and that's how I perceived myself. At the end, I was associating with the top half and felt more secure. Probably I was boorish.

There were of course positive aspects of the schooling experience, too, pride in grades, pride in being elected to office, in a few cases, even the joy of finding a friend and of learning. 'Most important to me were the people I met and the extreme pleasure of learning. . . . Niels Bohr's model of the atom, for example, gave me almost sexual pleasure.' (Male psychiatrist) Generally the men in this group had a better experience in school than the men whose wives did not work. Considering the small number of respondents, this may of course be a completely accidental contrast. Yet it is possible that the ability to make complex and unconventional rearrangements of their work and family lives was supported by a more positive and more secure experience in childhood and adolescence.[2] However, for many of the men and women in this group, too, schooling was something to get through in order to enjoy the later rewards of professional life.

I accepted what was said in school. One boy said he wasn't going to college. I couldn't have been more surprised if he said he was a Nazi. School ultimately led to success in life, an occupation which enabled you to have esteem, to be liked and admired by your contemporaries as well as being able to support your family. (Male doctor)

I would like to end this section on education with two quotes which underline the strong emphasis on competitiveness and achievement in American schools. The first is by a young lawyer; the second by a woman artist who spent some years in a completely non-competitive school in Switzerland.

I was and am very achievement-oriented. If you reach for the stars, you won't come up with mud. The higher ideals you aspire to, the more you can develop your potential. (Male lawyer)

In the school in Switzerland, there were real friendships. The kids were mature. You had total control over your lives. In America, there was competition for grades. My heart would always be pounding when I had to answer math questions or perform in spelling contests. In Switzerland, I never had to perform; I was never put on the spot. I loved science then, making models of planet systems outdoors. At the art school here, there was great competition. The girls were afraid to show their work, to share ideas. . . . They thought there was one answer. We competed for grades – there was also social competition. I felt the kids were less mature and isolated in the American system. I became grade-conscious. I rebelled against the discrimination, the fact that some kids were labelled stupid. (Female artist)

The original 'contract'

With the spread of the ideals of the Woman's Movement, many women felt it legitimate and desirable to return to work. How did their goals relate to what their husbands wanted to do? How were the husband's goals related to the professional development of the women? I tried to get a sense of why the women decided to continue in their careers and what the range of reactions from their husbands was.

In eight of the seventeen families, it was taken for granted from the beginning of their relationship that both husband and wife would work in their professions. For two of these men and one of the women, however, it was their second marriage. It is interesting to note that when the respondents re-married, they chose spouses with similar professional interests.

In one of these eight families, the woman, a psychiatrist, moved with her husband to a new city because they felt he had to establish himself in his profession and her work was more easily established in any large city. Despite the fact that this move made the continuation of her advanced training more difficult, I did not see this decision as more than the sort of compromise any two people who live together have to make. At the time I spoke with her, she was practising happily in her profession; he was an assistant professor whose tenure had yet to be decided.

In the other nine families, including six families where the wives had professional credentials, the wives clearly subordinated their professional goals to the needs of their husbands. They planned to stay at home when the children came; eight vaguely assumed they would 'do something' later on when their children were grown up. All but one worked outside the home immediately after they were married. The artist thought his wife would support them while he did his work. She left university after two years and moved to a new city so that her husband could do his graduate work. All nine women, in fact, moved so that their husbands could establish themselves professionally.

Why did the women who originally thought of staying home go out to work? In one case, the husband encouraged her to do so. Two of the women began working for financial reasons. Another was offered a part-time job. 'I knew I wanted to do something but I hadn't defined it yet. My children were very young and I wasn't interested then in a part-time job. There was a six-month trial period. I tried it and really liked the work.' (Administrator)

One woman returned to law school because her marriage was so different from what she expected. Her husband described it in the following way:

I had five years of practice before I married. Our house wasn't the little cottage she dreamed of. It was hard for me to understand why she was upset. I always came home tired but happy. She was unhappy here with the kids. Before we had kids, I came home late and wondered why she wasn't overjoyed to see me. I was tired. I wasn't gay at eleven and wanted to go to bed. She felt isolated. . . . Before going to school, she envisioned that we would have scholarly talks by the fire. At first she wanted to marry and have eight children but she's changed. She's disillusioned with the role – she did get neglected. She wanted the prerogative of having her own life.

Interestingly, despite their decision to stay at home with their children, several of the women found themselves keeping up with their professions. The artist continued with her painting at home. The wife of the orchestra conductor I spoke to, a singer, travelled weekly to New York with her little daughter to continue her voice lessons and performed regularly. The high school teacher had taught, even with one young child, while her husband was in the army and then was active as a volunteer and paid tutor until she resumed her professional work.

The women professionals said they made do in a variety of ways until they were able to resume full-time work. The lack of facilities for child care and the expectation that women would remain home wth young children, however, made it practically impossible for older women to pursue their careers without taking several years off to raise their children.

Once the women got involved in their profession, they became increasingly committed to it. One woman who thought of staying home with the children explained that although she worked at first for financial reasons, she found it more and more difficult to stay at home.

I decided to get my M.A. because I was afraid of falling behind my husband. That turned out to be the best year I ever had because I could make up my own programme. Before I went to work, I was hostile and murderous. I couldn't justify working and I couldn't justify staying at home. The feminist movement was beginning. At first I rebelled. It was threatening to have to work to prove something. I discovered it's no great honour. After my daughter was born, I didn't know why I went back. There were financial reasons. I also thought it was wrong staying home when you have an education. On the other hand, I wanted to stay at home with the infant. I wasn't happy either way. In the long run this situation was healthy; it made me think. I wanted my husband to tell me what to do but he didn't care. He said it's my life. Now I would be angry if he told me what to do.

The husbands' reactions to their wives' return to work
Some of the men had great difficulty accepting the fact that their wives were moving outside the house into the world of work; this was especially true for men who took for granted that their wives' primary concern would be the household. The first husband of the singer I spoke with who, at the beginning, was supportive of her work, disapproved when he realized she had to take more serious steps for her professional development.

In 1966, I had young children. I decided not to take the next step which was residence in Europe. My children were young and my husband wouldn't go. He wouldn't allow me to go. I didn't want to rock the boat – also, I felt that maybe my voice wasn't good enough.

She separated three years later and is now working full-time, teaching and performing. There are no children at home and her present husband is very accepting of her profession.

One professional man, who had encouraged his wife to work part-time and had accepted her full-time involvement, thought she had changed considerably.

At first I felt that here is an intelligent woman: she shouldn't be wasting her life. She'll be more interesting. Before we married, she wrote about devoting herself to me and just staying home. I said that was nonsense . . . but now she's become a different person. She's more competitive and career-oriented than I am. I'm more in the middle. She's oriented outside the family.

The professional whose wife went back to law school was very open about his mixed reaction to her decision.

When she went back to school, I agreed to be here at seven to eat with the children. There is a girl that lives with us who cleans and sits with the children. We are dependent on her. I worry about what we would do if something happened to her. My wife has an apartment in———where she can stay overnight during the week. I knew she liked to work outside; I thought perhaps in public relations. I thought law school was a lot for her to take on. After being out a long time, she might not have been able to do it. We took a woman into our practice who had been out a long time. It was a disaster. I also thought – and was afraid – she might like it out there too much. When your wife is at home, she is in a way your property.

Eight out of the seventeen husbands who met their wives in professional school or as professionals took for granted that their wives would continue to work. Aside from the problem of children, which I will discuss later in this chapter, they were used to meeting women who wanted to work outside the home and were ready to share the household work. 'The division of labour was natural. We both went to school together and both went through the same experiences.' (Lawyer) In fact, the woman doctor I spoke with said that when she thought she could not go on with her work, her husband encouraged her to cut down, but not to leave. Only one man objected to his wife's working in her profession. In this case, though, there were already children at home. 'My second wife continued working until her pregnancy was so advanced that she could hardly get up and down the stairs. She stayed home for a few months and went back to work, again. I'm not too happy about it because it's not good for the children.'

Later in this chapter I will explore further the range of advantages and problems encountered by people in dual-career families according to the men and women I spoke with. Even with the greater acceptance of the husbands who had met their wives as career women there were difficulties in their lives that were not easy to work out.

The situation at work

The work experience of these professional men and women was generally similar to the picture which emerged in the previous chapter from the interviews with professional men in single-career families; basically, the same issues and strains were reported: the tensions in the early stages of the career, the uncertain criteria for advancement, the importance of establishing the right social relationships, the feeling that one's personal needs were often not taken into consideration, and the competition among colleagues even after the professional was established.

For the older people I spoke with, however, it had been easier than for the younger respondents to find work. There were more opportunities and less competition. Some of my respondents, then, began their work lives with much greater security than others and they were very aware of the differences between their experiences and the experiences of younger people starting out in their professions. 'We went back to the city I was brought up in after the war and I went to the paper there and asked if there were something I could do. He said they needed a copy editor and I said I could learn it. So I became a copy editor. Now we have a, couple of thousand applicants on file for jobs.' (Male editor in his late fifties)

On the other hand, one of the older professionals took a position which for a long time did not require a doctorate but when he was about to be given tenure, there was more of a demand for formal qualifications. He had a long, tense period with disagreement among his senior colleagues and those in a

higher position of authority before he was granted tenure.
These observations suggest that the experiences of insecurity, competitiveness and pressures at work vary with the general economic situation and the demand and supply in one's particular field. In addition, there seems to be a trend toward formalization of credentials due to the expansion of higher education. For the women in my sample this meant that those who entered the work world in their professions after the children were older not only were behind in their professional experience but were entering a very competitive job market at an unusually late age.

Occasionally, women may have an advantage in finding jobs because of equal opportunity and affirmative action principles, but in the two relevant cases other factors worked in their favour, too. Two women lawyers were entering organizations committed to hiring women but one also had a speciality the corporation needed. The second woman had graduated from one of the top law schools in the country.

Women on the higher levels of an organization sometimes find they have to work very hard to establish their authority. If there is a man around, respect and attention may be directed towards him, no matter what her formal position.

One of the women is older and makes half of what I make. That woman worked for a man whose job I took. It's a challenge to win her loyalty. I will never have it to the extent her boss did. I want the office to function properly, though. They hired a man to work for me. The older woman looks at him as her boss. This all happened since the summer but I knew it was coming. (Female administrator)

Some professionals consciously tried to improve the atmosphere of their work lives by stressing co-operation. 'We don't want to be competitive. We take equal salaries. The new doctor will have one equal to ours in five years. We don't have to try and be protective of our patients.' (Male doctor) This particular doctor also talked about competition for influence and privileges in the hospital. It is easier to reduce competition in a small group where you are in control than in a complex organization. The music professor gave an example of consciously maintained co-operation.

There is a sense of integrity here. The three people who lead the choir, band and orchestra could potentially be terribly competitive. We help each other out, we maintain warmth at all cost. We give each other money for instruments if any is left. We send our players to help and set up; it could be the opposite. You have to think about these things in the long run. (Male music professor)

When it is possible to achieve a sense of unity, the people involved seem to feel good about where they are.

Generally, there is tremendous co-operation in the firm. Anyone will help you, no one wants to show you up. They are not very aggressive, not very competitive. They don't even like to fire people. When they had to fire their receptionist, it was traumatic. (Male lawyer)

Unfortunately, a few individuals acting in certain ways do not automatically change institutional goals. The overall policy of most work organizations emphasizes competitiveness rather than co-operation. The rationale is that the 'dynamism of American business derives largely from competition within firms', as an administrator of a major business school put it in private conversation.

Generally, the men and women did not seem as insatiable in their ambitions for their future as the men in the last group I spoke with. (See Rapoport and Rapoport, 1976, for similar findings.) A few worked as hard as the most ambitious professionals in the single-career families, but several men made some modifications in their schedules. These were minor compared to what the women arranged but they permitted them to transport their children to school and to devote more of their time to the children at home than did their colleagues in the single-career families. Still, the men felt more pressure at work than their wives to become successful and prove themselves. Although the women were ambitious, they were delighted to work well as professionals and manage their family lives as well. They felt they already had proved themselves by managing to become professionals. (See Paloma and Garland, 1971; Horner, 1971, and Rossi, 1965 on ambitions of women.) That does not mean that the women took any old job just to work. They were interested in good professional work even if they didn't feel the drive to be on top.

> I had an opportunity to take a job with less responsibility, with less prestige as someone's assistant. But I wanted these things, I wanted to be happy in a job. There's no sense working at a part-time job you dislike. I like this job. I'm the only lawyer in this department. It's prestigious – I have an expense account, I can use the dining room. . . . It's difficult to give up. (Female lawyer)

The female university administrator I spoke with, however, had experiences in shaping her development which made her more competitive and which were probably more similar to those in business organizations. She was not satisfied with her position. 'Eventually, I would like to run the division. The worst thing I could think of would be to do the same work for the rest of my life.' Among the men, only two were interested in becoming something more than what they are. Both were lawyers, interested in advancing politically. One had no children; the second, with three children, suggested that he has always had problems remaining in one work situation. 'I always put myself in a pressure cooker. I never had to move. I sought insecurity. I get bored easily.'

Both the men and the women were keenly aware that they had embarked on a new family style that did not fit easily into their work lives. The process of working out a multitude of arrangements involved continual change in an effort to create the right work–family balance in their lives.

The over-scheduled family

Both the men and the women spoke over and over again of the complications managing their jobs and taking care of the needs of their families. Nearly all had very difficult work schedules. When there were no children, the schedule of the husbands and wives was essentially the same. One couple worked at home together; two others, two lawyers and two people on a night schedule at the newspaper, often ate together in the city and came home together. However, in the case of the two lawyers, the wife often remained at home at night while her husband returned to work or attended political and community meetings.

Where there were children, it was generally the women who managed to arrange their work schedules so they could be at home to take care of the children and start dinner. The artist left her studio to be home when the children arrived; the statistician left her work at three p.m.; the school teacher was at home fifteen minutes before the children came. One businesswoman and the woman lawyer in a large corporation were home at four-thirty and five-thirty, while their husbands came home later. How do the women's schedules look then? 'I'm up at six-thirty and then come home at five-thirty and make dinner. I fall asleep at nine. When I don't fall asleep, I knit, watch television or read the *New York Times*. I can't get into a book. I sometimes start the dinner for the next night.' (Female lawyer)

Three of the women I interviewed were with their children at work when I came in; I never saw a child with any of the men I interviewed at home or at work. I would guess that the presence of children is much more frequent with women than with men. Occasional care of the child at work and less demanding time schedules may be accepted as somewhat more legitimate for the women professionals than for the men I spoke with. The leeway is narrow, however, and in some large organizations, a woman can neither deviate from the time schedule nor bring in children if they are dismissed early from school or if the baby-sitter does not show up.

That women adapt their work schedules is not a sign of low work commitment. They did, however, show a stronger commitment to their families than most of the husbands. The woman doctor said that unless they went away to their country house for the weekend, her husband worked continually. One professional married to a businesswoman had two children from a previous marriage. Together they had a third child; yet it was the wife who came home at four-thirty to cook dinner for the family and remained at home, frequently alone, with the children in the evening while her husband went to work or attended a political meeting.

Seven of the seventeen husbands adjusted their work hours somewhat to take young children to or from school. A few of the husbands, especially those with young children, were very concerned about the children and after a long working day tried to spend time with them. 'My husband comes home tired but immediately gets involved with the kids.' (Female psychiatrist) Although men with young children, then, do not feel able to make substantial changes in their work schedules, they do help with transportation and the care of the children when they come home. Unfortunately, their help was only a very partial relief of the burden of the woman.

The effects of work on the marital relationship

What do these men and women come home to when they return from work? Nine women walk into the house, relieve the part-time baby-sitter or meet their children coming home from school. They immediately start taking care of the children, doing household tasks and getting the dinner ready. Only three of the seventeen couples have housekeepers. One couple lives in a commune and four are without children at home. What kind of mood are they in then and what kind of mood are they in when their husbands arrive?

Those who have no children or have housekeepers at home found the transition from work to the household the easiest. That was true for both the men and women I spoke with.

Living in a commune means the housework is divided. We can go out if we want to and never worry about a sitter. The other day, my husband came home upset; we took coffee upstairs and could disappear without a problem. (Female assistant professor)

Several of the men reported that although they came home in a good mood, their wives often did not.

I come home high, worked up at times but feeling good. My wife is generally more melancholy. If she has a tense day, she feels sorry for herself – and can be fierce.

My mood is usually good when I come home; hers is usually not good. She has the stress of her job and the frustrations and then has to deal with the kids when she comes home. In sum total, though, she is better off than before.

Aside from those families with full-time housekeepers, what made for differences in the women's situations at home, in how they felt and in how burdened they were? If both husband and wife met in professional school and continued on in their careers or met as professionals, the sharing of household chores between the husband and wife was the greatest.

> He does what I ask in the house. He's co-operative and undemanding. (Female singer)

> He does more than I do. (Female lawyer)

> We share completely. If she were to stop working, I would expect dinner to be ready but we come home at the same time. I'm obliged to help . . . I'm a prudish [sic] person but I don't think I'm less of a man when I wash dishes. I'm comfortable. When we entertain, we do it together. I'm comfortable that way. (Male lawyer)

After they had children, most women arranged their schedules to be at home after their children came home from school, or as in the case of the mother of the infant, immediately after work. It was during this period, however, that even the women who met their husbands in professional school or as professionals received proportionately less help from their husbands than they did before the children were born. In one family, the husband thought that the sharing was about the same as it was before they had children ('Generally we share without discussing – like cleaning up after dinner'). The wife, however, believed that the greater burden fell on her.

> Dinner is never ready and my husband has a short temper when he's hungry. The cooking is all on me and he has strong food preferences. I would like him to take the kids and prepare dinner – and I sit down and watch. I have the kids the whole day . . . I also do most of the housework. I get the kids dressed and ready for breakfast. He drives them to school. I'd like him to do more . . . without my asking. When we talk about it, he does more. Each year he does more, but I don't always like to ask . . . I want to continue my studies. It will require a lot from my husband. He'll have to do more with the kids. I think he

may do it. He may not even get angry – but I'm reluctant to ask. I can't believe someone would do that for me.

The professional who had two children from his first marriage 'baby-sat' for his wife with their third child for several months until he started to work in a new firm. His wife now returns from work at four-thirty. He does much less now and does not like to 'empty the garbage, go shopping, stand in line or have the car fixed'.

The equality in household sharing is actually put to the test after the arrival of children. There is an increase in the amount of work to be done; children need attention and concern and they create obvious scheduling problems. This is also the point where traditional conceptions of sex roles maintain their greatest strength. Many professional women retain traditional feelings of obligation to their families, such as the woman who hesitated to ask her husband to care for the children in the morning. At the same time, traditional sex role expectations about men's work are perhaps even stronger. Most men see their jobs as more central life interests than the jobs of their wives. Their wives are working because they want to, but they, the men, have no choice. Furthermore, because conventional sex role conceptions shape expectations at work, most husband's jobs are less adaptable. Men are not expected to take time from their work to care for the children. Most men, therefore, feel they are simply not able to reduce their hours of work and come home early.

The problem becomes even more accentuated when the woman at first does not work outside the home or works part-time and then changes to full-time involvement in her profession. The husband is then used to the care the wife puts in the household, and many have difficulty taking on more tasks in the family.

I shop occasionally and fix meals. I hate picking things up. I'm sloppier and tolerate a mess more readily. My wife is exasperated and resentful when she comes home and finds the house in a mess. I get angry. She feels guilty. I do almost as much as she does, though . . . gradually and reluctantly I accumulated duties.

In three of the families, the wives stayed home until the children were older. The husbands did relatively little in the household and by the time the wives returned to work, there was much less for them to do than in a house with young children. The sharing they did, at least from the point of view of the husband, was acceptable to their wives. In one family, the wife did considerably more than the husband, even while working part-time and being active politically. Now that she is in a full-time job, he picks up their child and cooks the dinner each evening. Occasionally, he complains about it.

At times, the kinds of helping the husbands engaged in seemed to be nearly irrelevant if one considers the total amount of work that has to be done in a household. One professional, in a family where there was a housekeeper, said that he does jobs now that he has never done before such as picking up something from the drug store on the way home from work. He is also at home every evening with the children and is intensely concerned about them. He occasionally does some shopping and helps with the cooking when there are guests. 'My wife is really lucky I can afford to send her to law school and to have a housekeeper. Without the help, she wouldn't have been able to go.'

The mixture of reactions, the generosity and the selfishness that seem to exist in the same person, have to be understood in the context not only of the traditional expectations of male and female behaviour within the family, but in the context of the man's sense of pressure about his work; that for him, it appears, there is no choice; he has to work, he has to achieve, he has to be successful. Whatever else happens, this aspect of his being is a given and not a matter of choice.

It is not surprising that the women tire earlier than their husbands. The wife cares for their children and makes dinner; after the children are asleep, there is little energy left. The quality of their relationship together is greatly affected by her exhaustion. 'We always passed like two ships in the night.' (Female elementary school teacher) 'I fall asleep at nine and on weekends when we visit I'm ready to leave at eleven.' (Female lawyer) Where there are very young children, the time after dinner may be hectic until they are in bed. 'We both end up being very tired and feeling restricted.' (Male physicist in private industry) One woman said that when she has a tense day at work, she is especially tired at home. 'I come home exhausted and fall asleep right after dinner or I fall asleep and wake up. Then I can't get back to sleep again afterwards.' (Female administrator) The woman doctor I spoke to said that many women would simply not be able to manage all they had to do. 'I think women are taking on more than they can handle. I am really capable and I had so many difficulties. Some of them just won't be able to make it.' If women are burdened with the double obligations of work and family, their husbands seem to suffer from more psychic strain at work; perhaps this is because they feel so pressured to prove themselves and succeed. Tensions are especially great when there is insecurity, but also when the professional feels he has too much responsibility. 'I can't leave my work at the office. I'm frequently with my briefcase, worried and wanting to work. I don't relax well. TV is helpful but I'm a workaholic. It's hard for me to read the newspaper, no less a book.' (Male lawyer) The artist during his untenured years once had a lump in his throat for the two-month period in which he was unable to find a solution for the work he was doing. Two of the male professionals had heart trouble; they reduced their working schedules only after their second attack. Such psychosomatic symptoms were reported mainly by males. The two women lawyers felt nervous because of work pressures. 'There is constantly time pressure exerted by the clients and court which makes me nervous. I think this schedule will continue unless something traumatic happens.' (Female lawyer) Both husbands and wives reported withdrawal at times and short tempers. One woman said that when her husband was upset at work, he was violent with her, with the children and with his own mother.

The women, then, suffered from tiredness; they were moody, nervous and sometimes short-tempered. Some men experienced more severe psychosomatic symptoms; others withdrew from the family and were short-tempered with their children.

With the persistence of the traditional role conception of the women come concern and guilt about the well-being of the children. One woman said she was so worried about their baby being cared for by a stranger that they decided to let the baby sleep when they were out of the house and wake her when they returned. Later on, she travelled back and forth from her office during the day to spend time with the children.

A few of the women felt guilty about putting their creative energies into work and leaving so little for their families.

If I didn't have to worry about the future, I might not work. I'm tired. I'm upset with the kids. I put all this creative energy into school and I'm exhausted. My husband is more easy-going, more confident. (Female elementary school teacher)

I believe our problems in the family were intensified because I work. I wasn't there to do things. Sometimes I'm away on weekends and evenings. There are differences in the times I have with the kids. The traditional pattern is interfered with. In some ways, I regret not being there, on the other hand, if I were there all the time, I'd be more difficult to live with. On a four-day weekend, I go crazy. (Female administrator)

Some of the professional women found themselves paying far more attention to their children than they did to their husbands.

Occasionally, I concentrate on what he is telling me. The children want to talk and I think it's more important to listen to them. Once in a while, we'll linger over a drink and talk. I don't know if my husband realizes it but I'm more concerned that my time at home is with the children. They're in a formative period. My husband is an adult.

One woman suggested that although she received physical help from her husband, she sensed that in some ways she was not living up to his expectations of what a woman should be doing.

The man envisions his parents' marriage. There are more household things that he would like done. He would like me to provide a homestead for the child. I get physical support but not psychological support. He doesn't understand how exhausted I am. He would like me to be gay at eleven.

Another woman thought that greater adherence to traditional role expectations had rewards for both men and women. Since she had children, she practised in the afternoons at home:

I see more women who enjoy being at home. I didn't know women like that. This is the first time I have friends. I have more time . . . the mornings are relaxed. My friends' husbands travel; they stay at home, enjoy it and feel it's respectable. They are lucky and so are their husbands; it's less complicated. There is less to give when both people are working. Both need assurance and support that they're good. . . . The wife gets support from the husband's income. She's proud of the house and what she does. She gets support in her daily living. (Female psychiatrist)

Several of the men I spoke with thought their families suffered because their wives were not able to fulfil their traditional roles. One whose wife is especially involved in her work commented:

She is more committed to her career than I am. . . . The kids and the family suffer. I don't like the way they're developing, discourteous and spoiled. They haven't learned restraint. My wife became more independent. This has good and bad consequences. We are competing for the last word, the decision, the dominance over the kids. . . . Still, she is more tuned into the family than I am. She says it's because she listens. I am more of a disciplinarian. The kids are on her side.

One male lawyer thought that his wife's commitment to a career raised problems that were difficult for them to resolve.

I feel proud of my wife but I would like children. I'm not too excited by live-in help. Formally, she could take six months off after the baby is born although she says she can't. They like her and would be accommodating. I also feel her mother should come. We get along very well but my wife is ambivalent about it.

A young family requires so much; how can a woman be prepared to handle two things? If the wife is at home, she does more for you. It's better for the children, too. (Male lawyer)

Of course, the wash never gets done. (Male artist)

The husband who agreed to be home every night at seven said that even though he was with the children, he missed his wife: 'It's nice to come home and have someone here. A housekeeper isn't the same thing.' All except one of these men (the male lawyer) approved of their wives working. Their complaints centred around the difficulties they had when their wives did not fulfil traditional expectations.

What do you do when a kid is sick? Who calls the baby-sitter, who takes the kids to the doctor? Now it's more difficult with her working so many hours. I have to get more involved. It's easier for her to get a baby-sitter. We're dependent on cars, we both do the shopping. It's better to get help with the housework because if we do it, it takes time away from the child.

One man felt his wife became reluctant to do anything in the household.

I have asked my wife to be responsible for the housekeeper doing everything she is supposed to in the house but she would like to be relieved of that. She gets an allowance and pays all the bills which she would also not like to bother with anymore. Before, she went to cooking school, we had every French recipe there is. Now she doesn't want to cook a hamburger.

Five men out of seventeen seemed intensely tuned in to the family; four went into great detail about their children and the joy of the relationship they had together. These men were all in their fifties and sixties; perhaps at this stage of their life, their professional careers are put more into perspective and they are able to put energy into their families – or their children are older and easier to be with. Two, because of their wives' full-time involvement in their work, were forced to devote more time to their children than they had before. In both cases, there was a bit of tension between the husband and wife over the control of the children. One male professional said that before his wife went to work, he had much less to say about what was happening.

The father subconsciously is kept out of the children's lives by their mother. If that is her occupation, she wants him out. If the father participates fully in his profession and fully in hers, it downgrades what she is doing, that is, her role as mother. I go to the school conferences. My wife just heard what was great about the kids but I hear other things, for example, that one of our boys needs help in some area.

It is clear that some of the women had previously more traditional roles in the household and great control over the children. That control had to be shared when they were so involved in their own work lives they needed the help of their husbands. This issue does not seem to be a great problem for any of the younger people I spoke with.

All of the women I spoke with who still had children at home used up so much of their spare time for their families, they found they had no time for themselves.

If I had an hour to shut the door and be alone, it would be better. I rarely have time to unwind. . . . On weekends I do food shopping. When the baby takes a nap, I do what I can't do when he is around. It's difficult to do the womanly chores. I can't stand it when the house is in a mess yet I won't really clean it. In the evening, I would like to do something like pottery or swim . . . but it's not possible. (Female lawyer)

Sometimes on a hot day, I saw girls going to the beach and I wondered what I was doing and why I was doing it. I wondered again and again when things were difficult with the practice and the children. . . . My personal life is interfered with all the time. I arrange my schedule to be with the children. I don't remember having leisure, being able to do what I want. It's not strong in our family. (Female doctor)

In keeping with their somewhat traditional role orientation, the men felt freer going out in the evenings than their wives. Not only were the women more concerned with being with the children and getting some tasks done in the household but they were often too tired to leave. 'He is active politically and in civic organizations. Sometimes he goes to three or four meetings a week. I never attend more than one or two. . . . He enjoys his work. I have to relax more than he does.' (Female lawyer)

The women were ambivalent about what they were doing because they felt they had a choice; they could, after all, stop working and remain at home. However, they were not prepared to return to their traditional roles. They were not prepared to give up their careers even if there were no other institution or person to fill the gap in their families and households.

Most women had either never developed interests outside of their work or had gradually given up their other interests in order to devote their spare energy to the family. The two exceptions were the woman lawyer who did not have children and had time to enjoy 'feminine interests like cooking and decorating the house' and the assistant professor who received tenure without a doctorate and felt under no pressure to publish. If the others think of leaving work, there arises the problem of what they would do at home.

> Women who stay at home are groomed to stay at home. They fulfil their needs and their husbands' needs by doing home things. They resolved their dilemma. Now, I am so programmed to working, it would be hard to cultivate other interests. I could never get into cooking; I hate shopping. I couldn't do the expected things. (Female elementary school teacher)

> Five to ten years ago, I thought: Who needs this? I never had financial pressure. I did it in spite of it. Something is driving me; I don't understand why. It's hard not to continue once you've started. Now I'm delighted. I need it, I would be bored. I don't have enough hobbies or outside interests – and my staying at home doesn't appeal to my husband. He always hated my kind of woman. Even when I thought of stopping, he said, Cut down, don't stop (Female doctor)

The women thought they had more respect from their husbands because they worked as professionals and because they earned their own money. 'If the wife does not earn money, it has to be a really good relationship for that not to express itself in control.' (Female psychiatrist) 'I have more respect in the marriage because we both have jobs.' (Female lawyer)

Not only did several of the women I spoke with feel they had more respect from their husbands because they worked, but both men and women felt there was a better mutual understanding between them, that they were able to share similar interests.

> Working is better for the wife's development. If she doesn't work, she is like a flower that didn't blossom. You can easily outgrow your wife. I know women that worked their tails off sending their husbands through school. Then their husbands started associating with people of a higher income group. (Male lawyer)

> When my first wife worked, it gave her interests which she could add to mine. For example, we got friendly with delightful

people from Norway and France which she met in her laboratory. I would have never met them. Her return to work made our marriage better. (Male newspaper editor)

Those men and women engaged in the same or similar professions shared intensely with each other.

It's more like an urban homestead. If the jobs bring the people together, they will be more successful. Otherwise, they go in different directions. We both are interested in many of the same things, we both love politics. (Male lawyer married to a businesswoman)

We are both musicians. It would have been a great problem if I hadn't married a musician. She is talented, in many ways more talented than I am. She has written ten string quartets and composed many songs. . . . She plays the piano although she was never trained, and the violin. . . . Music has its own rewards. Although we have fights sometimes, she is empathetic. We will talk about musical problems and she knows what it's all about.

One woman suggested that she and her husband were so concerned with each other and so tuned-in to what the other was saying, that it was often the children who did not get the attention they needed. This was not a problem for the other men and women I spoke with.

If husband and wife shared professional interests, they expressed their common bonds more than those couples who were working in different professions. Two couples, however, were exceptions in my sample. Although in different professions, they shared an extraordinary amount. One was a psychiatrist married to a high school teacher and administrator. He was the oldest respondent I spoke with and through the years they developed many interests together, canoeing, bird watching, and an interest in minerals and geology. He read a great deal, painted and wrote. Compared to many other people I spoke with, I sensed broad concerns and commitments. The other was the couple who lived in the religious commune. Aside from sharing a wide variety of academic interests with each other, they both were committed to certain ways of living which demanded their energies and which at the same time provided a balance for their professional concerns.

As in the earlier interviews, there was often a carry-over from one's professional work to how one acts as a parent and spouse at home.

In my practice, I make decisions all the time handling patients. That all carries over into the family. I'm strong-willed and active, not a wilting flower. (Female doctor)

My job very much influences how I am in the house. I organize, analyse problems and make sure there is communication. Some women call their husbands when there's a leak; I call the plumber. A woman I know can't understand her insurance. All these things aren't a problem for me. (Female administrator)

In a few cases, the carry-over resulted in tensions between the men and women I spoke with. 'At home, I am intolerant of sloppiness and illogical statements. Things should be precise and correct. If my wife makes mistakes, I feel a need to tell her. It's a good way to start a fight.' (Male lawyer)

Earlier sociological theory has emphasized the potential for competition between husband and wife if both have careers and the disruptive effects such competition might have on family life. In fact this was one of the functionalist explanations of the predominance of single-career families.[3] Since many aspects of traditional role conceptions persist among the men and women I spoke with, one might expect that competition between husband and wife is a real problem in these families and that the wife's career is seen as a threat to the husband. In fact, there was little evidence of such problems. In only two instances did I get any such feeling; in both cases, the marriages had severe difficulties:

It's hard for a man. I was offered a job in a school he wanted. Three years ago, I changed from painting to sculpture. I didn't think it was good for one family to have two painters.

She is more independent. . . . Neither of us anticipated this. She has become more manly but she wouldn't have been content staying at home.

One man admitted that he felt envious at times of what his wife was doing and the man she worked for. 'Her work is more interesting than mine. She travels and meets people. I envy her boss and his facility for influencing people and getting things done. He's better than I am. He's a good administrator – and my wife is, too.'

Rather than competition, there appeared to be for some of the couples a tendency to lead separate lives. 'I do my own laundry, she does hers; we each do for ourselves. We get our own meals. There's not much we do together.'

In part, this situation develops because people have so much to do that they are not always concerned and tuned-in to what is happening with the people they live with.

> Often, instead of concentrating on each other, we think about daily pressures. These thoughts occupy our attention. If he tells me a story, rather than asking for advice, I sometimes tune out. He'll also switch channels. (Female lawyer)

> My wife talks more about her work than I do about mine. I don't travel around so much; it's not so fascinating. She's involved with details, though, and it's difficult to concentrate. She can rattle on, over-explain. I get bored and tune out. I tune out when she's talking with the kids – and other places, too. She has less trouble concentrating. . . . Each of us goes his or her own way. I don't miss it. If we had more time, it wouldn't necessarily be better.

For a few, there were personal differences which reinforced some separation. These men and women were brought up to believe that they would not be sharing their lives completely with the people they lived with.

> We're not indulgent about emotional problems. Sometimes I'm distracted when my husband speaks; sometimes he is. When I started teaching and brought problems home, he was not really interested. He had taught already. It was hard for me. (Female singer)

> When I realized I wasn't making it, I became nervous and started doing more sports – and not working as hard. I didn't discuss this at all with my wife; it was my own decision. (Physicist–private industry)

> It is good for us that my wife works. We each have a life of our

own. It makes her happier, satisfied. (Male assistant prof.–
natural sciences)

Since husband and wife both have 'lives of their own' outside the
house, neither feels the need to worry about the spouse being left
alone at home feeling abandoned. Being independent of each
other, they are freer to pursue their own lives. For those men who
want to devote even more time to their work than they are already
doing, having wives who are absorbed in their own work lives
allows them to turn their attention even more to their profession.

I get away easier to my studio because she is busy . . . although
she still complains when I work too hard. (Male artist)

Now that my wife is out working, she realizes it's not so easy to
simply close shop. . . . At home, I have a lot of reading that
occupies me. I welcome having the time to do it. (Male doctor)

It is interesting to note that even in dual-career families it is the
women who complain that they do not see enough of their
husbands. They seem to need more personal contact than the men
I spoke with. The women have reduced their schedules at work;
they rarely work at night. Their husbands, however, they
complain, continue to work too much.

Most of our fights revolve around the fact that we don't spend
enough time together. If I don't go back to work, I go out to a
meeting. If I work an hour or two after dinner, I'm more
relaxed. If my wife would take a vacation for a week or play
tennis at the end of the day, I would live in the office. It would
be a tremendous opportunity to get things done. (Male lawyer)

I would prefer my husband not to work in the evening. If,
however, he does more than he has to I get angry. After all, with
me, he can't just say he has to do that. I will scream. . . . But it's
like screaming to someone who can't stop, who doesn't have a
choice. If he has an emergency, I'm sympathetic and sometimes
go along with him to keep him company. (Female doctor
married to doctor)

I don't differentiate between work and family life . . . I work
all the time. My first wife saw it as a problem and landed up
with a psychiatrist.

Since the men feel more pressured to succeed in their professions, it is not surprising to find that they feel most personally happy when their work goes well. Three of the ten men I spoke with said that work gave them the most satisfaction in their lives:

> My greatest happiness is when I have an insight into my work after a struggle or when someone unexpected convinces me that my work has excited him. (Male artist)

> I am most content at night in the office when the phone isn't ringing and I'm getting my work done and when I'm involved in political battle, a campaign or fight in the senate. (Male lawyer)

Yet six men found their families a great source of contentment; they had older children or were personally involved in their care. Three of these actually spoke only of their families when I asked what gave them the most satisfaction in their lives.

It is remarkable that not one woman mentioned work alone as giving her the most satisfaction in life. Seven women did not refer to their work when they talked about what gave them the greatest satisfaction. Four men and three women found they were most satisfied when things went well both in their work *and* in their families.

> I am happy when the programmes I developed at work succeed and equally when everyone is enjoying themselves at home, when I go shopping with my daughter – or make a candle, when we go exploring. (Female administrator)

> I'm especially happy when things at work go well, when there are good results after an operation or interesting diagnostic problems . . . or when I have a close relation to the kids. That means a lot to me. They hang around like puppies. The kids always express their love but the other day my daughter expressed it in a special way that really moved me. (Male doctor)

> More than anything, I like to vacation far away. We don't do it often but the pressures are much more distant then. (Female lawyer)

None of the women wanted to give up her professional life. More than their husbands, however, they appeared to need personal contacts, a rich emotional life. Furthermore, the task of co-ordinating their work and family life was so great that seven out of ten of the women were most happy when they were relieved for a period from the struggle.

The effects of work pressures on friendships

Although it was not surprising to find that half the men I spoke to talked personally to neither their relatives outside the immediate family nor to friends, it was remarkable to discover that this situation existed as well for half of the women respondents! Both men and women in this group found it difficult to share personal feelings.

> I am a private person and not comfortable talking of private things. (Female administrator)

> I have no close freinds I would talk to about really intimate matters. I'm not even sure I would discuss certain things with my mother or sister. (Female administrator)

Several of the men and women said that they are simply too busy for friends.

> I have no close friends I would talk to about really personal problems, although I have a lot of friends. I'm not discriminating . . . I'm too busy, really to make friends. (Male lawyer)

> I have two friends I speak to but we don't have a lot of time for friends. We meet more people that we like but we don't take the time. We're too busy. (Male artist)

A few of the respondents spoke about the effect of competition on friendships. One was the musician who very consciously created a co-operative atmosphere among the people he worked with. 'If you're intensely competitive you're not likely to make friendships. It's hard to be friends if you're so up-tight about your career. You compare every review and applause.' Another was a university professor who had been very close to a colleague brought up at the same time for tenure.

> We both had young families. Our children played together. Now we don't speak to each other. The department didn't really want to give tenure to either of us. I wanted to go with my friend to the administration but he refused because he had more department support. . . . In the end, my work and what I had attained professionally got me in. . . . At a party, my friend's wife made it clear that she wanted nothing more to do with us.

Three of the women felt no need for friendships; they described their husbands as their best friends. Two of the older men said that they would share anything with their own children who now were married and had families. One woman, the artist, said that most of her friends are women because they can be trusted more than men. One woman did not 'allow friendships' because she was so unsure about whether or not they would remain in Boston. Competition, fear of confiding, of trusting, of losing out somehow, of using time for friendship that could be better used advancing their career were all expressed in these talks. That friendship is also directly tied into subtle class differences came out in conversations with two of the families I spoke with.

> We knew a couple very well but became less friendly because of economic and social differences. As their income went up, we could share fewer and fewer things with them. . . . We couldn't afford to take the vacations they did. Their philosophical attitudes also changed . . . from liberal Democratic to Republican.

Generally dual-career families reduce the formal entertaining they do.

> I am not a social person. I don't like parties. I don't want the fuss. Music has its own rewards. (Male conductor)

> We're so tired, we don't entertain. When we have time, we relax . . . but we do enjoy an occasional social evening with friends. (Male physicist)

Some of the women refused to do the work involved in having guests 'My wife will not entertain.' (Male artist) 'When my husband invites people, he cooks.' (Female artist) A few of the husbands found it difficult not to invite colleagues or to cut down on their visits to colleagues:

> We had to cut down on our social life. My husband hasn't been too understanding about that. . . . On weekends when we visit, I'm ready to leave at eleven. . . . My husband feels obligated to have his co-workers over and has many friends. Lots of my husband's friends aren't married and lead a different type of life.

> Once, when my wife had an exam, the dean of the medical school had a party and we couldn't go. I really regretted that but I would feel strange going alone.

> My wife disliked my colleagues and disliked entertaining. I would like to feel I didn't have to invite people and I didn't . . . but it has a great influence; it's much harder if you don't. We argued about it . . . I would socialize more if my wife were different.

Most husbands, though, accept a reduced schedule and are glad to have the additional quiet time. 'We're not going out so much to cocktail parties. We still go out, but not as much. Gradually, people stop inviting you. My wife even used it as an excuse to stop sending Christmas cards.'

Generally, then, formal entertaining was considerably reduced and so was close interaction with friends. It is possible that orientation towards a career has something to do with not feeling free to open up to other people and to form close friendships. A professional's general orientation may be so geared to furthering a career that control of emotion carries over into personal life and that he or she may fear admitting to weaknesses or revealing personal secrets. Among the men and women I spoke with, there were several examples of competition interfering with friendships at work.

The little time that was left over from work was mostly devoted to the family. Men, more often than women, engaged in activities outside the family but these were structured and involved purposeful activity.

Conclusion

Although dual-career families combined traditional with new ways of being together, in most of them there were attempts to discuss and concretely work out problems and to develop a shared responsibility for them. Some of the women waited several years to return to their professions; they had clearly subordinated their own professional goals to their husbands' and their family needs. Their husbands did not have to deal extensively with child care. If that were not the case, and especially if the wife had completed professional school with her husband and continued on in her profession, the care of the children and household were negotiated.

Most of these women were the first professionals in their families. Their mothers, most of whom were academically educated or interested, encouraged their daughters and were aware that they had not done as much with their lives as they could have. Furthermore, the Women's Movement gave the women I spoke with a sense of legitimacy for their personal goals. They did well in school, although some found the competition difficult to handle, and more than the men, reacted intensely to it, physically and mentally. Not only was there academic competition, but both men and women were sensitive to the social competition and class differences within the school.

Not all the women who stayed home with their children intended to return to work from the beginning. Some did indeed keep up professionally, by practising and performing, for example, while others returned 'accidentally' because a job was available, because there was a need for money, or because their husbands were totally absorbed in their own professions and too busy to pay attention to them. Once the women got involved in their own professions, however, they became increasingly committed to their work. While their husbands generally approved of their careers, several of the men had great difficulty in accepting the fact that their wives were moving outside the house into the world of work. This was especially true for men who took their wives' involvement in the household for granted, but even the younger men showed attachment to traditional aspects of the woman's role.

The younger professionals had and continued to have great feelings of insecurity, uncertainty about the criteria of selection, the feeling that in the process their needs as individuals are not taken into consideration. Women on the higher levels of an organization sometimes found they had to work very hard to establish their authority. Both husbands and wives had very difficult work schedules. Usually it was the women who managed to arrange their schedules to come home earlier to care for their children and start dinner. Where families had a housekeeper, a live-in student couple or a communal household, work and family arrangements were easier.

Generally, the men and women did not seem as insatiably ambitious for their futures as the men in my last sample. A few men worked as hard as the most ambitious respondents I spoke with in the last chapter and all took for granted their right to achieve as much as possible in their professions, but several made some modifications in their schedule. These were minor compared to what the women arranged but they permitted them to transport their children to school and to devote more of their time to the children at home than did their colleagues in the single-career families.

Tensions for the men seemed especially great with insecurity or overwhelming professional responsibility, and they reacted by physically withdrawing, moodiness, short-temperedness, even violence, and physical illness. Tensions for the women revolved around the long work schedules and the difficulties of combining their work and family life. They were often nervous, guilty about the children, moody and longing for some personal time for themselves. They were ambivalent about what they were doing, in part because they felt they had a choice and could theoretically stop working and remain at home.

Occasionally, the women spoke of the more peaceful and easier lives of the women they knew who did not work outside the house. Actually, that alternative was the prevalent expected role for middle-class women when they were growing up; it permitted them to withdraw from competitive and pressured behaviour. When these professional women, however, thought of possibly not working outside the house and remaining at home, they realized they had gradually given up all their other interests in order to devote their spare time to the children. Furthermore, they liked what they were doing; they did not want to give up their professional involvement. Both husbands and wives agreed that the women felt better about themselves when they were working and were therefore easier to live with. The women believed that having a profession and an independent income increased the respect from their husbands. The men felt that their wives brought new interests into the family that could be shared together; especially husbands and wives in the same profession shared a common sympathy and understanding for work problems.

The tenets of easier sociological theory emphasizing the potential for competition between husband and wife if both have careers and the consequent disruptive effects on the family were not apparent in most of my talks. Rather than competing, there was a tendency to live side-by-side, a tendency towards independence and a life of one's own of each partner. Furthermore, concern with pressures at work often made it difficult for professionals to pay full attention to what their partners were experiencing.

For those men who wanted to devote even more time to their work than they were already doing, having wives who were absorbed in their own work lives allowed them more freedom. Although their wives were understanding of the work demands they complained that their husbands worked too much and that they did not have enough time together.

Half of the men and women I spoke to had no close friends. This group expressed feelings of privacy and a reluctance to share intimately with others. They were too busy; they didn't feel the need for friendships. Competition, fear of confiding, of trusting, of losing out somehow, of using time for friendship that could be better used advancing their careers were all expressed in these talks. Two of the respondents expressed an awareness of the difference in economic resources which prohibited them from developing friendships with families wealthier than they were.

Formal entertaining was seriously reduced when the wife worked outside the household. A few of the men regretted not being able to socialize more with colleagues, which they found important for their professional development. Most, however, felt fine about the new arrangement and participated equally in the preparations when guests came.

Appendix

Notes on interviewing
In the last set of interviews with single-career families, some of the professional men were reluctant to spare time for an interview. In this set of talks, two male psychiatrists refused to make the time to see me. The woman physician never phoned back: I called her nine times before finally reaching her. One of the female administrators wanted to be interviewed during the afternoon because she planned to have lunch with her daughters: however, she refused to adjust her schedule so I could be home when my children came back from school. The other female administrator came an hour late for the interview after her secretary informed her I was there. She had forgotton about our appointment.

After our talks began, the women were open, interesting, and interested in the questions raised. They tried very hard to be helpful. The men were also more open than the respondents in the last set of interviews, though not as open as the women. Perhaps that was because having to work out family and work arrangements forced the women to think about these problems before I ever came to see them. Furthermore, the professional woman expressed her dissatisfaction with the traditional role and her husband had to deal with that, rather than to live as if there were no problems to work out. The interest and concern of the men in these problems led to interviews which were longer and more intense than those I did with men in single-career families and which were somewhat more similar to my talks with the East European males.

4 Does socialism make a difference? Dual-career families in the Soviet Union and the German Democratic Republic

Introduction

As work organization and attitudes toward work and family life are not isolated from the larger political and socio-economic structure, I decided to include a number of interviews with professionals from countries with structures quite different from those characterizing the United States. In particular, I am interested in the contrasts between socialist and capitalist societies. In this chapter, I explore the effects of school and work organization on personal relations outside work in marriage and with friends, in the German Democratic Republic and the Soviet Union. The first problem is whether these two socialist societies have at all succeeded in introducing a more co-operative orientation among the children at school. Secondly, I try to understand whether there is any continuity in this respect at the place of work after formal education has ended, in particular, whether professionals are involved in co-operative work groups with control over their own work lives. Thirdly, I discuss job security and other social supports, including those that make women's participation in the labour force feasible on the large scale that is characteristic of Eastern European countries. Finally, I make an effort to link what happens in the world of work to certain developments in the family and in friendship.

Perhaps it is helpful to begin with some comments on the historical and political background of the Eastern European interviews.[1] In all interviews which take place over a short period of time there are reflections of experiences of years of living and changing. Some of these important experiences that shape feelings and human relationships are particular to the personal

112

life history of the respondent; others are more shared, shaped by the political, economic and historical conditions of a certain period. These past experiences are reflected in the values, outlooks, and reactions of people not only to what they lived in the past, but how they see what is happening in the present and what they hope for in the future. I think that both the Jews who emigrated from the Soviet Union and who constituted the majority of my Russian respondents and the East German professionals I spoke with had such a shared past political experience which was crucial for their development and present perspective. More than half the Soviet Jews spontaneously mentioned sorrows and difficulties connected with the Second World War and with camps during Stalin's regime. A few had parents who were killed during the war by the Nazis; even more spoke of having parents who had been in a Soviet camp. Some parents died in camps, others remained for as long as twenty-five years. One woman's mother was in a camp for twenty-five years, her father, a high level party communist, was killed in a purge. The father of one of the people I spoke with, in turn, was the head of a Soviet concentration camp. Of the older people I interviewed, one had spent eight years in a Soviet camp and then was fired from his work during a purge. One physicist had seen twenty-two fellow students taken away; these are only a few of many incidents that were described. For many of these people, the fear of unpredictability remained; one could not be absolutely certain of not being picked up and taken away. This alienated them from their regime, from their nation; and because some thought that these experiences had something to do with their being defined as Jewish, they tended to have fears and to see their destinies as somewhat apart from those of other Soviet citizens.[2]

Nearly half the Germans I spoke with had fathers killed in the war; two women were in Dresden during the bombing of the city. One family had emigrated during the Nazi period to the Soviet Union because they were communists and then returned years later to Berlin. The deaths of parents of the East Germans were mentioned in a very specific context, as explanations of why they grew up in poverty. There was no self-pity; they did not seem to identify with the experiences of their parents.

Many Jews in the Soviet Union and East Germans experienced extreme poverty after the war. There were severe food shortages; thousands of peasants in the Soviet Union died of hunger. For those who were able to survive, there were less serious problems, such as being ashamed to go to school because of the condition of one's clothes. A physicist from the Soviet Union described the apartment he had with his first wife, a pianist:

> We lived with twelve other families in a common apartment with a shared kitchen and toilet. Our room was divided by a curtain; on the other side lived my wife's sister. When a woman came from the countryside to help with the child, there were five of us in the room.

I am describing this period for several reasons. The people I spoke with lived through these years, some started married life under very difficult conditions. Quite possibly, this contributed to tensions in the marriage which still continue, although in a less intense way. On the other hand, it was a period which many people then saw as the beginning of a new society and the way they looked at their lives in this new society and later on, the comparisons they made with what they had before, led to a positive evaluation of their present living conditions, especially by the East Germans.

One woman who is now a lecturer at the Humboldt University was the daughter of farmers. After the war, she was sent to a course for teachers for six months and that was the beginning of intense work in the communist party and her professional development as well. Now she had a large, sunny apartment and was preparing for a research year abroad. Another woman, now a journalist and studying for a more advanced degree, described the following change: 'Now we have a big apartment [it was a two-bedroom apartment]. We were so poor after the war, I could never believe we would live like this – I can have so many books.' I am not suggesting that there were no unsatisfied needs in the German Democratic Republic but rather that for many people, the housing, food and general economic situation had improved over the years and daily living had become easier.

The Soviet interviews were much more varied. Firstly, the people I spoke with came from different cities in the Soviet Union. In addition, they were comparing their present situation to what they had experienced in the Soviet Union, to what they hoped for in their new country (in part influenced by their observation of elite groups in Israel, Europe and the United States), and in some cases, for those who had left Israel for Germany, to their experiences in all three countries. It is probably fair to say that the widening of economic opportunities and the necessity of paying higher prices for goods and services put certain pressures on people, pressures to buy what it is possible to have. A psychiatrist expressed this feeling in the following way: 'You have to work harder to get something in Israel. In Russia the income differences and possibilities of buying are not so great, so you can't run so much.' His colleague also confirmed this impression:

Here [in Israel] the economic situation is different. Russians come from big, beautiful cities where there were not such differences. In Russia, there are not such rich people and no beggars. You don't notice such differences. Here they are so great – in clothes and education. There people were clean and serious. It is another spirit altogether.

The problem of being unsatisfied with what one has is a thorny one; it cannot be said that growing personal needs are restricted to people who have emigrated. In East Berlin, there is a constant comparison with West Germany; older East German citizens can cross over and many West Germans visit the German Democratic Republic. It is also true that there are differences within the society. Although some workers are extremely well paid, intellectuals as a whole are clearly a more privileged group.[3] In part, the lack of complaints about conditions had something to do with ideological conviction; it is equally true that in the context of the German Democratic Republic the people I interviewed were privileged.

Among the men and women I interviewed from the Soviet Union, there were varying evaluations of the standard of living before immigration. There were complaints about not having enough money, which directly affected what one did at work as well as the marital relationship. We will return to this issue in the section on work pressures. Although all people started households with limited private living space, by the time they left, most families had comfortable apartments; a few even owned cars and had household help. Several respondents mentioned problems of limited choice in food and other items and the long hours spent queueing or going from one store to the next hoping to find what one needed. On the other hand, there were some institutional supports in the Soviet Union, which will be discussed later, and which were lacking in their new countries.

Occupational origins of the respondents

Nearly all women work in the Soviet Union and in the German Democratic Republic. Both the need for human labour and ideological considerations have made work outside the home for women a normal aspect of communist society. Even the earliest communist theoreticians saw work for women outside the home as a solution to their bondage and inequality, although radical changes in the structure of marriage and family would also be necessary.

In the great majority of cases today, at least in the possessing classes, the husband is obliged to earn a living and support his family, and that in itself gives him a position of supremacy, without any need for special legal titles and privileges. Within the family he is the bourgeois and the wife represents the proletariat. In the industrial world, the specific character of the economic oppression burdening the proletariat is visible in all its sharpness only when all special legal privileges of the capitalist class have been abolished and complete legal equality of both classes established. The democratic republic does not do away with the opposition of the two classes; on the contrary, it provides the clear field on which the fight can be fought out. And in the same way, the peculiar character of the supremacy of the husband over the wife in the modern family, the necessity of creating real social equality between them, and the way to do it, will only be seen in the clear light of day when both possess legally complete equality of rights. Then it will be plain that the first condition for the liberation of the wife is to bring the whole female sex back into public industry, and that this in turn demands the abolition of the monogamous family as the economic unit of society.[4]

In Table 4.1, the professions and ages of the men and women from the Soviet Union are listed. In Table 4.2, the professions and ages of the men and women from the GDR are listed. About half of the men and women in the Soviet Union had mothers who

TABLE 4.1 *Profession, age, and sex of respondents from the Soviet Union*

Profession	Age
Males	
Dentist	40
Engineer	61
Industrial engineer	50
Pianist	38
Physician	47
Physician	42
Technical engineer	50
Physicist	56
Psychiatrist	28
Psychiatrist	43
Psychiatrist	62
Violinist	32
Violinist	47
Females	
Anthropologist	48
Industrial engineer	36
Fashion designer	58
Translator	36
High school teacher	36
High school teacher	37
Physician	47

worked. It is interesting that nearly all of the mothers were professionals, doctors, high school teachers, etc. The East Germans also reported that their mothers worked, but in no case was the woman professionally trained. These women, except for two farmers and one seamstress (the mother of an engineer who had immigrated to the Soviet Union during the Nazi period because she was a communist), decided to work only during the war period and immediately afterwards when they were the sole supporters of their families. The principle of work outside the home for women was not institutionalized until the communists took over.

Everyone in the Soviet Union and in the German Democratic Republic had a father who worked. In the Soviet Union, half the fathers had professional positions, doctors, engineers; I also include high-level politicians in this category. Among those fathers who were not professionals, there were many white-collar

TABLE 4.2   *Profession, age and sex of respondents from the German Democratic Republic*

Profession	Age
Males	
Educator and administrator	45
Writer	50
Composer	35
Composer	45
Engineer	47
Assistant professor	33
Females	
Editor in a publishing house	37
Adult educator	35
Industrial psychologist	33
High school teacher	
Journalist	37
Assistant professor	45
Graduating university student	30

workers or people who had their own businesses before and now were doing managing, bookkeeping or simply technical work (like watchmaking) in state shops.

In the German Democratic Republic sample, there were only two fathers with professional or semi-professional training. One was an engineer and the other an elementary school teacher in a small town.

The effort of professionals in the Soviet Union to have their children continue in professional careers has been observed several times, not only in my interviews but by foreign journalists as well as by Soviet politicians who wanted to balance the universities, and at the same time continue to receive support from elite groups.

In spite of a variety of 'loading devices', the children of professional people ('specialists') still have a better chance than anyone else of entering higher education. Actually, the most serious gap is not between the specialists and the rest, but between urban and rural children. One recent survey showed in the region under examination, 82 per cent of 'specialists' children who had finished the ten-year school went on to some kind of further education; the proportion for urban workers' children was 61 per cent, but for the children of peasants it was only 10 per cent.[5]

Since the need for professionally trained people in the Soviet Union may be reduced in the next few years, children whose parents have gone to university as well as those millions of youngsters who have completed secondary school will have difficulties continuing their education.

Although elites in the German Democratic Republic also want their children to continue in professional positions, there are rather severe regulations insuring that the children of workers are able to enter university. Although some professional parents were able to get their children into university, one young woman said: 'Because I went to university, my son won't be able to but I don't think it's all so important.'

Education in the Soviet Union and in the German Democratic Republic

What happens to children in school is not only shaped by the needs of that particular institution, by the interaction between teacher and student and of course among the children themselves, but also by the societal setting, of which the school is only a part. What is happening in other areas of society feeds and is fed upon by what goes on in school. 'Educational systems never exist in a vacuum, but are shaped and influenced by the conditions and needs of the societies in which they function.'[6] The very tenets of Soviet society are based on a belief that the environment shapes the personality and the values of its inhabitants and that the Soviet school has not only the possibility but the responsibility for contributing to the formation of its citizens.

Intelligence tests are condemned as 'bourgeois pseudo-science', while the whole concept of 'intelligence' as innate ability is viewed with deep mistrust. The Marxist believes that human nature is not basically pre-ordained, but rests in the hands of man himself; the Soviet educator accordingly regards the child as much more malleable than do most Western educators.[7]

One Soviet teacher complaining about the problem of achievement of the children put it this way: 'There are no bad children, only bad teachers'. A Soviet mother pleased with this conception of the child compared her son's experiences in the Soviet Union to what had happened to him in Israel.

If a student in the Soviet Union doesn't study well, the teacher is questioned. Here they tell you, you need a private teacher.[8] That would never happen in Russia. There, the teacher is constantly in touch with you; you can come in the school anytime so you know the position of your child. Here, they're more independent and that's good, but they're still children.

Soviet educators not only believe strongly in the importance of school environment but believe Soviet parents have important contributions to make. Makarenko discussed the relationship of the family to Soviet society.

Our family is not a closed-in collective body, like the bourgeois family. It is an organic part of Soviet society and every attempt it makes to build up its own experiences independently of the moral demands of society is bound to result in a disproportion, discordant as an alarm bell. . . .

You have joined together in goodwill and love, rejoice in your own children, and expect to go on rejoicing in them. That is your own personal affair and concerns your own personal happiness. But in this happy process you have given birth to new people. A time will come when these people will cease to be only a joy to you and become independent members of society. It is not at all a matter of indifference to society what kind of people they be. In handing over to you a certain measure of social authority, the Soviet state demands from you correct upbringing of future citizens. Particularly it relies on a certain circumstance arising naturally out of your union – on your parental love.[9]

Because family and the school are seen as two institutions working together to help form the child, it is expected that parents and teachers will co-operate closely. This is indeed what seems to be happening, both in the Soviet Union and in East Germany. An East German teacher of twelve- and thirteen-year-olds, listing the innumerable extra activities she was involved in, included some comments on her work with parents. Although parents and teachers generally work much closer together than in the United States, the teacher also had a familiar complaint.

I am a class leader. There is one for every class. I have to visit every house of each student in that class at least once a year so that one evening each week I am with parents – but when a child has problems I have to go four or five times. Then I can't visit every family. Then there is the parent council. Everyone thinks they have something important to say about education – they would never speak to a doctor that way. . . . The director, if he's smart, can regulate this. In every class, there are five to seven parents responsible for the development of the class. This year half are men and half are women. They not only help me with hikes and celebrations but also with problem children and their families. We come together once a month.

Since it is the environment, rather than heredity, that is seen to shape individual personality and ability, all children in the German Democratic Republic and the Soviet Union in the first years, ideally attend the same school and are not segregated according to ability within the school.

Not only does the Soviet system reject the segregation of pupils into grammar-school-type courses and secondary-modern-type courses, but rejects any kind of segregation within the school. Every class is thus expected to have a complete cross-section of ability, from the brilliant to the plodder, all doing the same courses at the same pace.[10]

That does not mean that teachers have no sense of differences in student accomplishment in the classroom. They are, however, pressured to have every student adequately complete the year's material. In addition, there are some specialized schools for artistically gifted children or for children particularly talented in mathematics and languages as well as for children with severe physical or emotional handicaps. Some Soviet parents mentioned the different reputations 'normal' schools have which make the better ones more attractive. Generally, though, the uniformity of school quality and of the curriculum is much greater than in the United States.

Because there is an interest in studying for a profession and an awareness of certain advantages of intellectuals both in the German Democratic Republic and the Soviet Union, the child is aware of how important it is to do well in the classroom, as well as he or she is able to. Although there is such a stress on achievement, there is at the same time a co-operative orientation. How is it possible to have these exist together? Perhaps it is better to think of the values as existing side-by-side. As an East German woman put it: 'Children are confronted with the collective experience, but the pressure to achieve is great; so they are presented with different values.'

Children may be responsible for everyone in a row and the rows in the classroom may be working against each other. They may co-operate in classes and compete against other classes or compete as children of one school against children of another school. 'We see here reflected the influence of a well-known principle of dialectical materialism: Conflict at one level is resolved through synthesis at the next higher level.'[11] Such 'socialist competition' is not only used to encourage individual achievement but to insure order, discipline and conformity in the classroom, and later on in the society.

> Since each child's status depends in part on the standing of the collective of which he is a member it is to each pupil's enlightened self-interest to watch over his neighbour, en-courage the other's good performance and behaviour, and help him when he is in difficulty. In this system, the children's collective becomes the agent of adult society and the major source of reward and punishment. The latter typically takes the form of group sanctions expressed through public criticism and, ultimately, the threat of exclusion from membership. The individual is taught to set the judgment of the group above his own and to subordinate his interests to those of the collective.[12]

A Soviet woman made the following comparison: 'In Russia, the children are more disciplined. In Israel, the children are free. It is good and bad. It is rather difficult because they are too free. They have no manners and discipline. It is better to compromise.'

On the one hand, sometimes the pressure of the collective can be very hard on the child who fails. People who have been brought up in children's houses in the kibbutz have also mentioned problems of labelling a child or defining a child in such a way that some of his or her potential remains hidden. On the other hand, helping the child with problems may mean a 'saved soul'. An East German teacher working with adolescents made this comment: 'If a child gets into trouble, he gets work, he gets into a collective, he is never abandoned. That doesn't mean he's never lonely – that we all experience – but he has the possibility to develop.'

Although many people did not think that students helped each other greatly, others said they were divided up into neighbourhood groups and did homework together. The better students are expected to help the poorer ones. 'In school, it is necessary to finish the year, no matter what. The better people are supposed to help; if they don't want to, the students get together to speak with them. It is necessary to help. The teacher may give extra lessons.' This respondent from the Soviet Union said her child did not get comparable help at the University of Jerusalem.

> The Russian students feel alone, not at home. In Russia, people help you. If you have a problem, you get help all the time.
>
> In school we had many groups, also an amateur theatre group. We learned much together; it was always taken for granted that we support the poorer students and learned with them. There were many competitions among the different classes. Still, it was all very different from here [West Germany].
>
> What I see as really positive is this education towards a sense of community and to have this collective experience already as a child.[13] (East German editor now living in West Germany)

Not only are the better students supposed to help the poorer ones but the older children are expected to take responsibility for the younger ones.

> A fourth-grade class 'adopts' a first grade class in the same school; the older children escort the younger ones to school, play with them in the schoolyard, teach them new games, read to them, help them with schoolwork – in general, act as older brothers and sisters. Moreover, the manner in which they fulfil

this civic responsibility enters into the evaluation of their total school performance as a regular part of school activities.[14]

The co-operation in the classroom among students is not as extensive as many teachers hope for. Nevertheless, the stress on co-operation and responsibility for others does seem to create a different spirit than children in most American schools experience. An East German educator expressed the following views:

> The youngster who only works for his own achievement is looked down on in the classroom and is not respected. But even for getting into university, grades are not enough, although necessary. . . . But then not every one wants to get into university. Students are suited for different things. An intellectual isn't something special in this society.

Actually, even in this particular interview, inconsistent attitudes towards the worker were expressed. It is obvious that intellectuals have advantages in the society. In this case, the respondent admitted he would not want to work in a factory and that he tried very hard to make sure his daughter was accepted into the university. At the same time, there is little doubt that the worker is much more respected than in the West.[15] This connection to the world of work begins very early in school. 'Each school may also be a "ward" of a shop in a factory, or of a bureau of a municipal agency, with the workers devoting their spare time to activities with or in behalf of "our class" at the neighborhood school.'[16] These activities bring the children into the world of work rather than isolating them from it. In addition, it is hoped that through these visits, the proper social attitudes will develop. An East German woman now living in West Germany said that her children have very different experiences than she had growing up in East Germany: 'Once a week we went to a factory to work. At the age of fourteen I spent the summer working in a chemical factory. I learned what work means and never look down on a worker.'

All children, ideally, experience not only the world of the worker but some of the pleasures traditionally reserved for the wealthy. Several respondents mentioned that their children took music lessons at the schools. Even if a child continued privately, which seemed to be the case for a few of the Russians I spoke with, they had opportunities to do some beginning work in school. There are also club houses where children go for a variety of activities. 'My son could study, do chess or threatre. For ballet, one paid practically nothing. Once they worked on the construction of an airplane. There it is free, here [Israel] it is expensive.'

Eventually, children go into vocational school or into an academic school and prepare for the university. The period before acceptance into the university is an especially tense one. Grades are important; membership in a youth organization is too.

Many students want to study, but everyone has anxiety.

I wanted to study dentistry, but my grades weren't good enough.[17]

I had to take the tests twice. Not only was there competition but it was the time of demobilization and soldiers had first preference.

Nearly all the respondents felt that once they were accepted, there was no competition and that anyone who studied well could graduate.

In some fields there is less competition than in others; in some years it has been easier to enter university than in others. In the German Democratic Republic, generally, there are still many professional positions open which reduces competition. When one of my respondents, a Soviet physicist, finished high school in 1936, he could enter university without an examination. 'At that time, anyone who graduated with top grades (5 in each area) could enter university. It was called the "golden diploma" ' One doctor who later became head of a hospital department in the Soviet Union only studied formally until the age of twelve because of the war. He then studied on his own, took the examinations and was accepted into medical school. An East German engineer said that in his city there was a need for people who could do engineering work. 'I applied, got in without difficulty, and received a grant to study full-time.'

Generally, the state in socialist societies spends a great deal of money on education. A Soviet woman made the following comment: 'Everyone can study and it's paid for – and the education is much better because the state is richer and can afford all sorts of things. It's harder to become a doctor but everything is possible if one has talent and wants to study.' One Soviet engineer remarked, 'Everyone who does well can get an education. The students live well with a grant. It's after it's all over that the hard life begins.'

The encouragement for studying exists even for students who have a trade. There are correspondence courses and night courses to improve qualifications which many people take advantage of.

In Khrushchev's day, strong preference was given to *stazhniki*, people who had worked for at least two years after leaving school. By the early 1960s, the proportion of *stazhniki* was running at about 80 per cent; the remaining 20 per cent who came straight from school were mostly mathematicians or physicists.[18]

In the German Democratic Republic it is required by law to allow workers the necessary time to attend classes and examinations, although in actuality the combination of work and study places great demands on the individual who attempts to do both. I will come back to this problem.

A few of the professionals I spoke with had other occupations before starting university. Most of those who made rather radical changes in their careers were women. Their experiences are in marked contrast to those of American professionals who generally do not have other occupations before professional training and work.[19] Table 4.3 shows those Soviet and East German professionals who had been trained for other occupations.

Some of the encouragement to go back to school came from heads of departments where the respondents were employed, with promises of better positions afterwards. An East German journalist finishing university described her career: 'I was secretary in an art centre [a centre for cultural activities of all sorts] and I was told to get an education and that I could then do administrative work.' An art teacher described the changes she made, encouraged by cultural administrators interested in the development of art. Her employers were not quite so enthusiastic.

I left school after nine years, went to work in an office and attended school two or three days a week where I learned sales and book keeping. I then worked in a bank but I drew and the

TABLE 4.3 *Present and previous occupations of professionals who changed careers*

Present Occupation	Previous Occupation
Males	
Engineer	Factory worker
Engineer	Metal worker
Females	
Industrial psychologist	Technical draftsman
Editor in a publishing house	Sold tool machines
Humanities (*Kulturwissenschaft*) – last year of study	Secretary
Art teacher	Office worker in a bank
Journalist	Worker in a bookstore
Translator	Did light and colour control in a film studio
University teacher	Elementary school teacher

GDR wanted to encourage folk art. They organized a festival and I contributed some things. It was junk [*kitsch*] and so were many other contributions but they had nothing else at the time. They had and I believe still have continual seminars for fourteen days in folk art. I went often. Legally I was able to, but naturally the bank didn't like it so much because they needed the workers. I was asked to work as an assistant in an art centre in my area. I organized seminars and also took part in them. I had no education and felt insecure. I could have gone on to become a cultural functionary but I liked to paint and such things so I decided to become a teacher.

What are the consequences of not getting into university or of not getting a particular job? The above examples indicate that returning later for higher education is an actual possibility. Several of the respondents who tried to get into university immediately after high school had to make second-career choices either because they were Jewish or did not get the necessary grades. Since my interviews were with professionals, these changes were engineering rather than law, education rather than dentistry, etc. Nearly all of the respondents were very interested in what they were doing and committed enough to have 'no regrets'. I did not meet anyone who was not satisfied with his or her profession; however, I did not interview non-professionals so that I could not catch examples of unachieved professional goals. For the people I interviewed, opportunities for further education, the many work opportunities available and the feeling of self-respect that most of the people expressed seemed to be related to their general satisfaction.

Supports in socialist countries for working men and women

The Soviet emigrants and the citizens of the German Democratic Republic experienced peculiar tensions and pressures in many areas of their lives. There are for example frequent confrontations of East Germans with the citizens, and therefore the different social system, of West Germany as well as the tensions and non-predictability of living in an authoritarian state. Along with these problems, however, special advantages exist for workers in the Soviet Union and in the German Democratic Republic. Socialist societies have many supports for working men and women; both the Soviet emigrants and the citizens of the German Democratic Republic I spoke with were proud of these.

The guarantees of employment, education, medical and old age care are well known; they are crucial for feelings of confidence that there are certain levels below which one cannot fall unless one is a political nonconformist. The Russian emigrants who had left the Soviet Union were often tense about their future in these respects. The implications for the lives of those citizens who continue to live in communist countries are many.

In those areas where there is competition, to do doctoral work in the university, for example, or to get a desired job or promotion, I had the impression of more relaxed attitudes towards the outcome.[20] Such attitudes can be related to the perceived consequences of not achieving higher goals, which are not seen as devastating by the people I spoke with.

In high school and in university there was no competition; the competition came at the point when it had to be decided who went on for the doctorate. Still, it wasn't a problem because everyone could get work.

There were only two scholarships given for doctoral work in

the department but I was not at all concerned about getting one because I would have got a very good job anyway.

When I finished my training as a secondary school teacher, I thought I would have to continue teaching younger children because of a lack of jobs in my area. It didn't matter, though: the pay was the same.

After graduation, students are assigned a job which means they need not worry about where to find work. Some, however, are tense about being sent far away from where they live, especially if they have to separate from their husbands or wives for long periods of time.[21] When this happened to the people I spoke with, they were able to somehow manipulate the bureaucratic decision after a while and remain, return or move to a more favourable location.

The university finds you a job afterwards. I got out of that because I was afraid of being sent to a place I didn't want to go to – I told them I needed an operation, which was true, and also that there was no place in the Cribbe [day-care centre] for my child so I wanted to take a year off and stay home with him.

My first job was 4000 km away from my husband's. After a year I left to go to the town where my husband was. I found work there, too.

Sometimes a move was made to advance one's career.

After the conservatory, I had to go back to the town in the Ukraine where I was born but after a year I was invited to an academy in a larger city. The head of the 'music college' was a kind, understanding woman who immediately understood such a small place was not for me and signed the forms releasing me. Without these, I wouldn't have been able to leave.

It is possible to change one's work; it may be difficult to get housing in a new city but respondents changed jobs several times without moving.

My first job was in a project bureau for electrical work. I worked there for five years but was bored. Once I get into something and really learn it, I lose interest and want something new. I asked for different work and went into an electrical research institute. (Engineer)

Once accepted into a job several respondents commented on the help they had got. 'If you need experience, which you do at the beginning, doctors will help you – or if you have problems at work, you can take courses. You have time – you have your job.' (Dentist) This dentist also approved of how his staff was evaluated. 'In Moscow, a three- or four-man commission came to control, but they came as colleagues. They wanted to be sure everything was in order, which is the way it should be.'

Most professionals felt there was no competition because each person had his or her own job to do; generally, I did not get a sense of unlimited ambition except within the party and the university where there were some possibilities – and interests – in making spectacular careers.

> Our situation is different than at the university. There everyone joins the party and makes a career. In our school, the teachers do different things. Sometimes someone boasts about how good they are but they get nothing for it – respect, but nothing financial. Most people don't want to be directors. It's hard administrative work. (Teacher in high school)

> There are no intrigues or tensions in our organization, unlike a lot of others here when colleagues decide who's promoted. That's because people have specialized tasks.

When one's work is visible to others, there seems to be an increased possibility of competition. In the university, for example, there is team research connected to concrete issues and societal problems which need attention. Colleagues work on related problems and perceive some differences among themselves. However, the general atmosphere at work for most of the people I spoke with was not competitive.

Salary rises occur for most professionals at definite time periods and, except for a few privileged people who negotiate separately as individuals, are centrally determined for everyone at a certain level of experience. There are employees of large organizations, such as engineers, who do have tensions relating to payment of premiums; I will come back to their problems. For other professionals, the relative standardization of salaries reduces tension and competition among colleagues.

There is a joke told in Israel about the complaints of a Soviet worker which gives some indication of the supports Soviet citizens are used to. Asked whether the worker wanted to be part of a large work organization or set up shop independently, the Russian decided to open a shop. He was given the space and provided with tools. Soon, however, he had a complaint: the Israeli government had failed to supply him with customers. The risks and insecurities of self-employment are virtually absent in the Soviet Union.

Aside from outlandish personal behaviour or open political deviance, an employee is rarely fired.

In Russia, there is no official tenure but you stay once you're in unless you're always getting into fights or are overtly involved in political action. Every five years there was a new evaluation in the academy with an announcement in all the papers of Russia but they don't like to take strangers and usually don't. (Musician)

It was very rare for someone to be fired and that is not easy to do. There was a work committee which would inquire about the reason. (Fashion designer)

Most respondents mentioned that if people do not work well, they get help. Often mistakes are overlooked. 'First of all, if someone doesn't do well, it takes a long time to notice. If he has to move down, he often collects the same salary.' (Engineer) This kind of information is difficult to substantiate; for our purposes here, however, the perceptions of the respondents are significant.

With a non-competitive and helping atmosphere, a feeling of doing important work, a relative standardization of salaries and the life-long security of the position, it is not surprising that the colleague group becomes an important social group; this is formally encouraged, and from my observations, it seems that the work collective does constitute an important part of the professional's life, including the professionals at the university I spoke to.[22] The husband and wife are encouraged to participate in the work collective together. 'I must have my work

collective. . . . We go together to the theatre and outings.'
(Journalist) 'I studied ceramics with my work collective; when they
gave it up, I lost interest.'

The attachment to the collective is not without problems. One
woman described her husband's former work collective
negatively: 'The collective can have a good or bad influence. My
husband was once in a collective that went out drinking three or
four times a week. It was terrible. Now he is in a good one that I
trust completely.'

The professionals I spoke to believed they were doing important work; some of the research the sociologists and the industrial
psychologist worked on was requested by party heads. On the one
hand, the control and concern limits certain kinds of research. On
the other hand, professionals feel they can sometimes influence
policy. One woman worked on tasks requested by the state. She
had to mediate between important and influential groups of
people who had different approaches in industry in order to get
something accomplished. A sociologist described his department's research this way: 'Our sociological research is very much
connected to the party. The regime looks at everything and we
work on particular problems.'

Perhaps it seems strange to think of a high level of culture as a
support for professionals but many respondents spontaneously
mentioned the importance of literature, music and the quality of
education, not only for their lives but for what their children
experienced.

> The cultural life is far superior in the Soviet Union. The
> children are brought up in a healthier way. There are few
> criminal films or pornography on television. The children read.
> They are much more intelligent than German or Israeli
> youngsters of the same age. The education is much better.

> I went to America when my husband played in some concerts
> organized by Jewish organizations. These people were not
> cultured. In Russia, the Jews are cultured and interesting
> people.

> Russia is more cultured and that influenced the child.

In part, feelings of cultural deprivation come about because
immigrants are so absorbed in learning the new ways of their host

society, in and out of work. Several Soviet Jews living in Israel said that they were simply too exhausted to go out in the evening. In East Berlin, aside from great pride in music, literature and art, there is a great affection for the old buildings, the remaining traditional architecture. Tourists visiting East Berlin often find it poor and grey; they would be astonished at the enthusiasm of the East Berliners I spoke with who felt they were participating in and living intensely with a rich past and in a present vibrant artistic milieu which had cultural links to other East European countries and the West.

Finally, and very important for the problems and issues I am looking at in this study, is the support these regimes give to working women. The most important legal measures of the German Democratic Republic affecting women are:

1. The principle of equal rights (for men and women) that is firmly anchored in the constitution and in all subordinate laws.
2. Special welfare measures for mothers linked to an extensive health programme as well as accident protection, child support and pregnancy vacation.
3. A new family law which declares as invalid all parts of the old civil code hostile to women.
4. A new educational system that is intended to eliminate all educational limitations affecting the working class and especially women.[23]

Working women get a total of twenty-six weeks as paid vacation with the birth of their child and can take a year off while retaining their job. With the birth of their second child, they are paid for the whole year. When they return to work, they must be given a position equivalent to the one they had previously.[24] In addition, women who have had children outside marriage are able to get new apartments and their children into Cribbes faster than other women. That means they are soon able to continue working and do not have to worry about not having enough money. One woman who had a child outside marriage said:

> The father officially recognized the child and sent me money. I was treated so warmly by the director and my colleagues; it was as if the child were a child of the school. They visited me

often and brought gifts. I got a new apartment and was joyous. The medical care was good, even better than in Berlin because it was personal.

Several women, married and unmarried, had children in Cribbes after a few months. According to William Mandel, the nurseries in the German Democratic Republic are the best in the communist block.[25] However, not all areas have nurseries and not all nurseries are good. Foreign visitors to the German Democratic Republic have commented on the rigid programme in the Cribbes. Furthermore, there has been a great deal of public discussion on whether nurseries are the proper place to socialize children (Lapidus, 1978, pp. 133–5). Sometimes mothers, both in the Soviet Union and in the German Democratic Republic, prefer to take care of their infants themselves. Also, especially in the Soviet Union, grandmothers or older women often help out. Without the aid of grandmothers, many of the families would have had tremendous difficulties.

We would bring the child to the nursery or one of the grandparents would.

From '53 on, until leaving, my parents came to live with us in our six-room apartment. My mother did the housework.

My wife's mother travelled an hour and a half every day, each way, for years to take care of the children.

My grandparents brought me up. My mother was free to run around, go to the movies, do as she pleased. She could never just sit at home.[26]

There were also husbands who took over many of the tasks of child-rearing because their hours were more flexible. Generally, however, there are many more opportunities for children to get good care in nurseries in the Soviet Union and in the German Democratic Republic than in the United States.

Although certain aids do not eliminate all the household tasks, they are at least some relief from a few traditional chores. There is, for example, inexpensive laundry service. For most people, the main meal is eaten in school or at work, in canteens or inexpensive restaurants. In the evening, it is the custom to serve only a light meal so there is no need for long preparation of meals at home, although some families prefer to prepare a full dinner. Both the men and women I spoke with ate out often, usually with colleagues. I also observed many people in the German Democratic Republic going into restaurants alone. It was accepted practice to simply seat them at a table with others. Again, I spoke with professionals; it is possible they had greater access to certain machines and services than other workers (Matthews, 1972, pp. 97–107).

Role conceptions of professional men and women

All the women I spoke with took work outside the household for granted and would not consider remaining at home with children for several years.

> In order to feel good, work is important. It is bad to have to remain at home.

> A woman has to participate, be a part of life–then they both give. She has money of her own; it gives her dignity. . . . My family is important but I can't live without work.

> I would go crazy staying at home. My job was so wonderful. . . . I travelled all over the Soviet Union and to other countries as well.

> I want to work now. If I remain at home, there's no life left.

> It's like a dream to be working again.

In spite of this appreciation for work, the women saw themselves as having the main responsibilities for their families. The Soviet emigrants thought of this traditional role of the woman as more of a natural division within the family than the East Germans, but women in both countries were very concerned about their relationships to their children. The main concerns of Soviet women were the early care of their children (few were in nurseries) and the time they were able to spend together; the East German women, although finding the nurseries good, also were bothered by the limited time they had with their children.

From the beginning I paid more attention to the family. The family for women is more important than work. For a woman, it is her nature. (A Soviet woman)

I was able to do both the house and work but I know there are problems with the children—perhaps because I wasn't with them enough. (A Soviet woman)

My only problem is not having enough time for my daughter and I feel very badly about this. (An East German woman)

As my child grew older, it was harder. I left him in school until 5 or 6 in the evening when he was seven and eight but then it was boring – the after school programme wasn't good. Friends of mine then came to care for him or I sent him to friends if I had to go away. I am still very concerned that he is still so much on his own (the boy was ten). He calls me at work as soon as he arrives home; I leave him a slip of paper with his chores for the day. (An East German woman)

Some women, although certainly not all, complained that their husbands were not helping enough.

The husbands don't help. If they do, they get little respect. . . . The Soviet Union is a combination of an industrialized and very traditional country.

He doesn't help in the household; he doesn't do anything really for me.

From the men and women I spoke with, I understood that there were many conflicting attitudes and expectations which were being expressed. All the men I spoke with had professional or working wives and thought it important that women should be working. A psychiatrist from the Soviet Union who said that women had too much to do did not think that women should remain at home. 'A woman can't stay in the house the whole day and not work. It would drive her crazy.' Even the most traditional respondents recognized the importance of work for women. I include one such view although it is two-sided; the housewife's concerns and problems are simply dismissed as trivial.

It was impossible when my wife stayed at home. She did the

housework, attended to the child, read a little and gossiped. She had few interests and they were unimportant. If the child got a cut, she was all excited. When my wife went to work, I became really interested in her problems. The woman must work, not for a salary, but for her interests.

In many cases, the husbands help shop, prepare meals and in the German Democratic Republic a few men even clean. Some of the men care for the children. The contribution of these men should not be underestimated even if they do not live up to ideals of complete equality. In the Soviet Union, where attitudes were more traditional, the problem was often handled by hiring other women to work. Still, the wife usually had the main responsibility for the household and the care of the children.

My wife is in a theoretical field and writes books. She also cleans the house and makes the food. We had a four-room apartment. . . . My wife's task is to raise the girls, to make everything nice. It's the story of the world that the wife does these tasks—it's the atmosphere.

An East German raised in the Soviet Union and now living in Berlin thought he was more traditional than German husbands:

I think there should be automation for cleaning the windows, etc. but not that the man should do it. In Russia, the men are more conservative. Here, just because the woman has equal work doesn't mean she's the same as a man. She's still the mother—that's natural.

I clean certain parts of the apartment but my wife does more in the morning and has more responsibility. . . . I don't even notice that the dust is around until it really gets bad but she wants it clean. Those are male—female differences.

The sociologists in the German Democratic Republic I spoke with suggested that when women marry they accept the traditional roles but later on they demand more equality at home. The man may react angrily to the new relationship in the house and if he cannot accept it, the marriage may break up. My impression was that East German men, even while retaining some traditional attitudes, accepted the legitimacy of their wives' demands. Soviet men recognized the burdens of their wives but often did not see the solution involving their equal participation in household tasks. The conviction of German professional men and women, supported by frequent public discussions of this issue, in the long run has had and I think will continue to have tremendous impact on the future of equality between men and women in the German Democratic Republic. As we shall see, it makes a tremendous difference for the self-conceptions of German women.

The world of work

In several areas of work in socialist countries there seems to be far less tension than in the United States. It is rare for a worker to be fired; he is helped if there are problems, encouraged to continue schooling in order to improve his qualifications and given organizational time to do so. Because there is work available and specialization of tasks, competition seems to be minimal; workers become friendly and participate socially and culturally in worker collectives; many projects in organizations and universities are co-operative enterprises; there appears to be a great deal of common decision-making. These are not minor advantages; they are crucial supports for the men and women I spoke with. However, they do not give a complete picture of what happens at work. There are problems and tensions; some are only slightly aggravating, some have a tremendous impact on the individual and on family and other personal relationships.

A few of the respondents spoke of the first months of work as being a time of particular tension because of their anxieties about succeeding. These feelings seemed to be stronger and longer for my American respondents, but they definitely existed as well for some Soviet and East German professionals.

At first I was anxious about my work because it was all new. The students were sixteen and I was twenty-one; they used my first name although normally they would use both. The director came to observe once every two weeks; I always hoped it would go well and it did so there were no problems. . . . I always had to have my timetable. (Teacher)

The hardest part for me was when I started to work. I came with theoretical knowledge but it's different when it has to be put into practice. I had to ask questions all the time and from people in a lower position. When I was secure in my work it got better. (Engineer)

At the beginning you compete to get your work accepted. Once that happens, it is much easier . . . perhaps a publisher will ask me to write about a certain theme–or I write and hope it will be produced. (Writer)

In three cases, the two East German composers and a Soviet violinist, the anxiety about their work continued after the first year. One composer had great difficulties getting his music performed although the quality of his work is now established.

I've had a few pieces played here but mostly I am unrecognized. I sent my work to the radio, symphony orchestra, etc. For years they didn't answer, even if I wrote and asked them. I don't live close to the city and only come in every two months. Once I had to get my scores back in person. The secretary said they weren't there but I went to the cupboard and took the scores out myself.

The anxiety is always there but it is worse in a new situation. You don't know how you'll be accepted. (Violinist)

In all three cases, I had the impression that the difficulties were related to personal or political issues rather than to musical ability and acceptance. Several people I spoke with mentioned the importance of these if only to indicate that one had to be aware of them.

A few people thought it necessary to invite directors over in order to advance professionally; still others spoke of special problems at work, in two cases with women whom they accused of being prima donnas. A few seemed to have exceptionally good relationships with their directors and, as I said before, found their work collectives to be an important part of their lives. 'I was really friendly with my head and was invited to her house for Easter. She came to our house for the Jewish holidays'.

It is sometimes extremely difficult to draw the line between personal and idiosyncratic animosities and political conflict; personal jealousies or simple neglect may be covered over with communist cause excuses or subtle or not so subtle suggestions of politically incorrect behaviour. Uwe Johnson in his postscript to *Ich bin Bürger der DDR und lebe in der Bundesrepublik* refers indirectly to this problem, using examples of opportunists who mouth certain lines but act differently and officials who supposedly act for the public interest but often press for particular, non-public interests to suggest that silence about these issues brought about a dishonesty in East German society, a living as if everything were going on the way it should be. In the early years of the German Democratic Republic, some people were reluctant to see these problems because of their fundamental trust in the society.[27] In my talks, there were a few cases where the respondent felt accused unjustly of politically questionable behaviour. A violinist said the leader of the symphony orchestra he played in was jealous of him and spoke to the authorities:

> . . . perhaps suggesting I would remain in America; so I wasn't allowed to travel there, although I had been there before – and without being given a reason why.

> During the time I was teaching I was denounced by a student for not following the party line. I had good relationships with students and found the work simple. He didn't say what I was accused of.

> A work of mine was supposed to be played abroad; neither the other musician nor I could get out visas so the concert was called off.

> The hardest period for me was in 1952. I couldn't find work. Someone said I belonged to a counter-revolutionary organization. But then everything was fine.

Sometimes an individual whose relative landed in prison for anti-communist activity was also suspected of engaging in politically deviant behaviour; in that case his position at work might be endangered.

Even if there were no personal danger or tension at work, some of the Soviet respondents felt that political considerations guided their evaluative reports. I cannot be sure how typical these complaints are, how often such incidents as those mentioned by the Soviet Jews take place in the Soviet Union. The Jews have a somewhat marginal position in the Soviet Union; in addition, the men and women I spoke with were emigrants. The inherent bias of my Soviet respondents was an important reason for my decision to speak with East Germans. The concrete frustrations which contributed to the decision to emigrate were quite varied.

It was an impossible job; I was intensively involved politically. Two and two may add up to four but I didn't know if it should add up to six. The statistics don't mean a thing. For example, suppose we have to reduce the electricity by 1 per cent. I reduce it by less than 1 per cent. In order to get the premium for everyone I have to make it look as if it's reduced by the proper amount. If I don't do it and there's no premium the director will tell me to go. If I then look for another job, they'll call up my old director who will say that I'm an honest guy – two and two always add up to four, no matter what. . . . Then they'll tell me to come back in a month.

In my company I was supposed to give a critique to the director, but since they were trying for a special prize I actually had to submit two papers. One was an official evaluation that was good; the other a criticism that was bad. I thought Russia would fall apart economically.

A head of a department had the following complaint: 'A woman had hung up a picture that was something like an icon. She was not religious, but for months I had to go to meetings because of it.'

As Jews, many of whom had experienced dismissal during the Stalin period, my respondents were very much aware of their outsider position in the Soviet Union.

There was an administrator – a very bad man who was not only in the KBG but also in some camps. However, he married a Jewish woman. That gave us a little more protection.

It was difficult to work with the administration. They were anti-Semitic although they didn't say it. . . . There was espionage. Everything was read. I was afraid to open my mouth.

I was told that the Jews who work here can stay but that I couldn't hire any new ones. They told me there were too many Jews already.

One of the psychiatrists I spoke with believed that Jewish men conformed more generally in their professions because they felt like outsiders. I think that was also true for the Soviet women I spoke with.

> There were only two Jews in the organization. It is known that they work extra hard in order to keep their jobs, but for a woman and a Jew it was fantastic work.

> As a Jew you have to do especially well – and keep your mouth shut.

Feelings of being an outsider or of having to do especially well may exist even when the people one actually works with are friendly and non-threatening. Many of the Soviet Jews said their Jewishness made no difference at all at work. Still the past of Jews in the Soviet Union and occasional incidents in the present presented them with uncomfortable possibilities.

For those who engaged in semi-legal enterprises the threat was ever-present. Many of the respondents said that because they didn't earn enough money they had to do double jobs or work extra hours. Most of this extra work, although terribly time-consuming, was legitimate. For example, a doctor may take work in a second hospital. In two cases, dentists had private clinics in their apartments. One was an official clinic, one of the few private clinics allowed: the other was not an official clinic. Both dentists were continually worried about them.

> I needed permission every year to keep my clinic going. . . . I would invite my director who had the connections to the right people – you need good relationships. Still I know they would close the clinic some day and then I wouldn't have enough money.

> My husband had private patients which wasn't allowed. He was always worried about it but we needed the money.

Generally, the demands of the work situation do not fully take into account the needs of the family. Although some non-professional working women had reduced hours as a result of public discussion of the over-demands on women, judging from my Soviet and East German cases professional women did not.

(See also the discussion of Dunn and Dunn, 1977, on the working hours of professionals in the USSR.)

This is not to suggest that these demands should be seen as hovering over an unwilling worker: especially for professionals in both societies the personal commitment to one's work is intense. 'There is not an outer pressure but an inner demand to respond to the demands of the work situation.' (East German sociologist) Part of the commitment of some of the Russians and many of the East Germans included, however, their participation in building a new society. Their work was of central meaning to their lives; they believed that what they were doing was important, that they were making a contribution.

My work is most difficult because on the one hand there is a problem of building a communist society with the special relationship men should have to their work, according to Marx, and the pressures to achieve in industry.

Several years ago, I had an attractive job offer in West Germany but I refused. I wanted to bring something beautiful to the people. . . . For me, my work is most important, to make a contribution to my society; I couldn't just live a personal life; it would be boring.

Our work, our revolutionary work, our building up of a new society was the content of our lives. Through our work, we made many friends, had many gatherings. . . . We didn't want to concentrate on making our apartment beautiful, on the old family structure.

Even for those who no longer believed the system was worth working for, there was an intense commitment to what they were doing.

I love my work – I want more time to read, to be more prepared. I'm interested in everything connected with art. . . . I like to speak about my problems at work.

I worry and sometimes don't sleep at night thinking of my patients. . . . The most important thing for me is my work, if the operation succeeds.

> I couldn't live without my work. Without my family, life would be hard – I could live but badly.

In Russia, among high-level professionals, the problem is absorption in work.

> For me, my music is everything. . . . I have an inner drive to work, produce and compose as well as an outer pressure . . . to prove I'm good in order to get my work accepted.

What is wrong with such commitment? Why should it be a problem rather than a source of joy? I think it is fair to say that for most people work is both. Problems arise because work takes so much time and energy that little is left for other things. If work takes time and energy, it is therefore true that most husbands and wives spend time and use energy away from each other. Aside from normal study and work routines, East German professional men and women often spend a year in another communist country as part of their training. The year is spent alone without one's family, in part because of housing problems in the host country. This means that the husband and wife live separately for a year. In my sample, only the husbands were abroad; some Soviet women spent a long period of time within the Soviet Union away from their husbands immediately after they completed their professional studies. Most women, however, remained at home with their children.

> After my studies were completed I spent a year in the Soviet Union. . . . Everyone must do that before they are allowed to teach in the university. My wife was teaching and taking care of our two children.

One can ask what the problems are of living separately for a limited period of time. As we shall see, even a year had important consequences, according to the experiences of my respondents.

Even when the family lived together, time problems remained. Tensions over getting concrete tasks at work done in time seemed to be the most overwhelming pressure at work; this pressure existed even when the deadline was collectively set by the workers, which often was the case.

> If the required amount isn't done, there's no premium. (Engineer)

At work [here she is speaking of all workers, not only professionals] there are deadlines, time limits – all these cause stress. This is especially difficult for older people – they can't take it. (Industrial psychologist)

It was my hardest year at work. We set a time for when our team research was to be completed and all kinds' of commitments came due . . . I couldn't even work on my *Habilitation* (second thesis) I had so much to do. (University professor)

There is a difficulty when the collective decides on a deadline and you have to make it. The different groups in the collective must work together and if one misses the deadline everything is messed up and then you're criticized. (Engineer)

Our main tension came when something had to be delivered quickly and we didn't have the material to make it with. (Fashion designer)

Even if there are not time deadlines, professionals often feel they simply have too much to do.

At several points, I travelled to do two jobs. It must have added up to six years. I was glad because we needed the money, but it meant I was away a lot and came home exhausted.

Usually, the demands on professionals went beyond their actual work duties. These included doing one's own work or research, attending party meetings, teachers meeting with parents, etc. Two descriptions of the activity of teachers (one is now doing educational administration) indicate how overloaded professionals can get.

I was a teacher in a high school for several years but I finally had to give up. . . . I taught history and my demands steadily increased. I had great contact with students, I wrote articles on educational issues, I met all the parents; it is customary for the teachers to visit the home. There were teacher meetings, party meetings; I had no definite break for lunch. Students were constantly coming over to me. I left the house at six and had twelve hours of work with practically no free time – and then at night I had to correct papers.

I work six days a week but only four hours on Saturday. My schedule is crazy. In the morning I teach but then I meet a group of teachers for art. Every two weeks, I work in a pioneer organization. I'm a leader of the union in my school. There is party education for every leader because you're a party official. I also go to school to further my education in art. What gets cut is preparation. At night I work while my husband watches television. Another problem is that no lecture period can be cancelled; so if a teacher is sick, either a teacher has to run between two classes or someone has to step in, which I do at least five hours a week. Because of my union work, I'm supposed to have free hours.

In addition, many women go back to school to improve their qualifications. They work full-time, take correspondence or part-time courses and in addition have family responsibilities. I found this to be particularly frequent among my East German respondents. Women take advanced education later than their husbands, at a time of their lives when they are already quite busy. They feel completely justified taking this time 'for themselves'.[28] While the women may have started their marriages with some traditional patterns, as they get more absorbed into their work, meet different colleagues and become more independent, they demand more equality both in their lives outside and inside the home. Yet these interests in education and personal development take time; they add new demands on an already strained 'time budget' of the couple.

We were really busy because of my concerts and because my wife, while working as an engineer, decided to go back to school and become an English teacher.

Because my wife studied after work, I had to be in the house more.

My wife said to me, 'Now I want to improve my qualifications. You should do the same for me as I do for you.'

The man may have great difficulties accepting the changes of his wife especially if he has to take over more tasks in the household. 'Although I work at home I often have sudden appointments. My wife comes home after a long day and finds the household chores not done. She gets angry'.

Having different schedules may also put strains on husbands and wives.

> My wife was a ballerina. She danced with the Bolshoi ballet. It's impossible to be married to a ballerina – that's no kind of life. She had a tight regime; when she was at home, she had to put her legs up in a certain way. After a performance, she was exhausted. The profession itself interested her. We had no private life.

> My first wife worked for the television station. She had all the responsibility for the co-ordination of the programme. Everything had to be ready at exactly the right time. She also travelled a lot where there were outdoor programmes in certain villages and televised them on the spot. We had two young children who had to be taken to the cribbe every day.

There are differences between being employed in an organization where hours and responsibilities are more directed and working alone or in a university setting. Flexible time means the possibilities for time out are greater; when these are different for husband and wife, there are feelings of uneasiness.

> Wife: 'I'm so tired at night. I have to get up at six. He can stay up late and regulate his own schedule.'
> Husband: 'Both of us think our work makes the most demands on us.'

It is clear that the concrete demands of the work of husbands and wives are often incompatible. The consequences of these demands and absorptions in work result in difficulties which men and women are not really prepared for. Personal needs are only partially taken into account by child care centres, canteens, etc.; other problems remain which are a burden for both husbands and wives.

The effects of work pressures on personal relationships

Both the Soviet and East German respondents spoke of having real and good friendships; the Russians, particularly, perhaps because of their positions as outsiders in a new country, were nostalgic about the intense relationships, the good evenings of discussions and music that they shared with people they were close to in the Soviet Union. Actually, a retreat into personal and family life seems to exist in both countries. People have given different explanations, ranging from retreat into the family as an escape and resting place from work pressures and political anxieties to more time and material possibilities for husbands and wives to concentrate on themselves and their households. The return to the family may be viewed positively or negatively, according to one's conceptions of what the relationship between one's personal and public life should be. Aside from moral – political judgments, however, it is quite clear that the family in socialist countries will not return to the form it once had and that the pressures on family relationships in communist societies cause tensions which affect the quality of the time family members spend together.

After work, men and women spend time in queues hoping to find the goods they need; they may have to travel far from their work to their apartment. Children are picked up, the evening meal is made, homework has to be supervised, some household tasks taken care of. Especially in the Soviet Union, the woman has the main responsibility for these tasks; however by nine, often both husbands and wives are exhausted. 'One is good for nothing – not as a woman either; we are exhausted and irritated – not good as a parent.'

Irritation from exhaustion and irritation because of not finding what one needs may lead to arguments in the family. 'You can say they are unimportant but in the end they add up.' One complaint concerns the lack of money for what one needs. If the man takes two jobs, working in two hospitals or having a clinic at home, he is even more exhausted.

In Russia there are money problems and people are nervous about it. They're nervous because there's not enough help. They're irritated and not nice to their husbands and wives.

In Russia . . . the pay is bad. Food is cheap but other things are too expensive. It takes a month's pay to buy a pair of shoes and a month's pay for a vacation. They give you some pay but it isn't enough.

Often husbands and wives argue about what the money should be used for.

> Problems in the family come from the money situation; there is the war of where the money should be spent – I'm always tired from thinking about the money and what I need.

> At first G——decided what should be done with the money – books! Now we each have our own money and I buy clothes if I want to – I don't think that's superficial.

Although money problems seem less of a burden in East Berlin, one woman thought that the competition with West Berlin made some people dissatisfied.

> As a result of the competition with West Berlin, the living standard and the increasing needs of the people have developed. For us, at the beginning, fashion wasn't important. Now it is – and machines, too, although research has shown that many of the mechanical devices don't shorten the work load because of the preparation, cleaning and repair work involved.

Discussion about increasing 'wants' is frequent among the intellectuals I spoke with (compare also Brown, 1979). I heard the following argument between a husband and wife which brought out some of their other tensions as well.

> Husband: 'Despite material comforts, people are still unsatisfied. They always want more – they are so close to West Germany'.

> Wife: 'It's natural; people's desires are always increasing; there's a need for aestheticism and beauty. You lecture too much – you know everything of course'.

Problems of exhaustion and money are made even more delicate when there are sexual difficulties; from my respondents, I gained the impression that especially among Soviet professionals, but also among their East German counterparts, these are not discussed openly. A Russian musician noted that ' there is no Freud, no psychoanalysis – We didn't speak about such personal things; the atmosphere is different than in the West.' A survey in the Soviet Union of young married couples 'showed that more than a quarter of the men and half of the women in the sample considered their sex education insufficient or non-existent'. (Heitlinger, 1979, p. 185.)

> Many families had sexual problems but didn't understand them and didn't speak about them. Men never spoke about them to each other. I knew about my friend because she fell intensely in love with someone else. We gave each other hints but didn't speak directly.

> One problem we had was different sexual needs. Especially when they were seen as a duty I was turned off – when we had an especially nice day or at Christmas or after a concert, but not every night or two or three times a week. After all, when one is married a long time, one knows one's wife's body.

A Russian woman indicated that because the woman works so hard, she doesn't have time to care for herself, to make herself attractive for her husband. Fatigue affected the personal lives of many of the American and East European couples; for those Russian families sharing apartments during the early years of marriage, the lack of privacy was an additional aggravation.

Because of exhaustion, but also because of anxieties, political anxieties, anxieties about being Jewish, anxieties about deadlines, anxieties because of being overburdened, professionals in the Soviet Union and the German Democratic Republic are sometimes very nervous at work and at home. The tenseness, the nervousness may take many forms, ranging from more yelling in the household to more serious physical and mental reactions.

> When it was quiet and good at work, it was quiet and good at home . . . when it wasn't good at work, it wasn't good at home. Here [West Germany] it's more quiet; you're not nervous and you don't fight as much.

> When it's hard at school, I'm all right with the child but I scream at my husband or my mother. When he's in a good mood he would take it all right but otherwise he would scream and we would end up fighting.

In those times when I had to make a deadline I would come home nervous and tired. Little things could start a fight.

I'm already nervous on Sunday before the week begins. My husband complains I flare up easily. My son's birthday fell in June during the marking period; the last time, in the middle of making a cake, I slapped him. I went in immediately to apologize but he said it'll soon be better. He was understanding and encouraging.

If my husband asks me to do something extra in the morning I explode because my time is all planned.

A Soviet psychiatrist said that because Jews conformed more in their professions as well, they are often more nervous than other people. 'They are often angry with their wives and children and have psychosomatic illnesses.' One might explain the same symptoms without recourse to increased conformity but as a direct result of worries and fears about an insecure ethnic status.
    Both women and men seem to have had intense reactions when they felt there was too much to do.

I'm desperate. It's true I get four days a month off from my job because of my studies but then no one does my work so I have to do it – I just completed one year but I have four years to go. I don't know how I'll do it.

I don't mind working. I'm active but it's too much and I'm nervous. Teachers have the most breakdowns.

I was a teacher for several years but I finally had to give it up because of stomach trouble. . . . As a teacher my demands steadily increased. First, my contact with students, articles on educational issues, meetings with parents . . . teacher meetings, party meetings.

Here again, pressures are not only coming from the outside but from incorporating as one's own the ideals of the teaching profession and those of the community party.

I worked in an office from 1970–3. From 1971 on I went full-time to work and began university. The hours of work were long, seven-thirty to four with much travelling. I took the child to kindergarten and was on the go from six-thirty in the morning until six-thirty in the evening. Every two weeks I went to school for two days – I was allowed that. I drank tremendous amounts of coffee, got stomach trouble, had heart trouble and had to take three months off.

It is different to have to work for economic reasons than to have your economic security and work for pleasure. I was tense and in 1953 got ulcers. It was all too much for me.

Aside from stomach problems, alcoholism seemed to be prevalent in both countries. One woman professional described the reactions of her former husband to pressures at work: 'I married someone who was in the Academy. His reaction to stress was to drink; that is a problem although not publicly recognized. I thought of it as a weakness. Instead of dealing with the problems he drank and then the problems built up and got worse.' There seems to be an acceptance of heavy drinking, especially in the Soviet Union, where it is traditional. Although it cannot be assumed that drinking is completely related to pressures, drinking frequently and heavily may cause strains in the family.'In Russia, there is a problem of drunkenness. You're expected to drink vodka, in restaurants, at the house where you entertain important people. Without that, you don't advance. I couldn't stand it. If one in the family is willing to do it and the other not, there are problems.'

Tension becomes even worse if a person feels he is not succeeding at his work. This was an acute problem for one of the composers I spoke to. The difficulties in continuing to compose, being poorly paid and not fully recognized not only depressed him but led to difficulties in his marriage. 'My wife's musical taste has developed in response to mine but for me my work is all important and I am frustrated in my attempts to realize my ambitions. Women don't like men who aren't successful; it's a completely different relationship.'

Husbands and wives are both tired and tense from pressures at work. However, if the wife stays at home to take care of the children and the husband is away the whole day, the situation may become even more extreme. One initial reaction to the daily separation is described by a young woman who had been a student and who was now studying part-time and caring for her child. 'We used to spend all our time together. The first day he went to work I wept. It was a separation in our lives.' A Soviet woman said that the main problem of professionals is absorption in their work. The husband often is not able to fulfil all of his wife's expectations.

My wife says now she had no life. I worked every day until eight, nine or ten, came home exhausted and often had to work at night. Sometimes on Sunday, I worked with the director when we had to write something. I had no time for my wife. Leaders work very hard. We have to do research and attend all sorts of meetings; we find it difficult to get the things we need.

Even if the woman works she may have to live with a man who is more absorbed in his work than she is in hers. 'The women are tired; it is difficult to arrange everything. Often the wives find someone else who isn't such a great professional but will pay more attention to them, with whom they can live.'

A frequent complaint about the modern nuclear family is that when the man leaves the house to work, he is no longer directly involved with his wife in activities for the common good of the family even if he does bring home a pay cheque. It seems that this particular problem is relieved if the wife also goes out to work; however, the relief, the solutions bring with them their own problems, their own pressures on family life.

Both husbands and wives go out of the house to work; in most cases they get involved in usually different worlds, different atmospheres, different friends, different pressures and problems, different spirit of life perhaps. In socialist countries, I am not only speaking about the normal work day but also the union meetings and party obligations which take time and take husbands and wives away from each other for even longer periods. Because the demands of work are concrete, often time-determined, because the consequences of not working well are not only disturbing but have practical impact on one's daily living, both men and women respond to the demands of work, leaving family relationships for energies and hours left over. The respondents cared about both their work and their families but if the absorptions in work were too great, there were effects on the family many of the respondents found difficult and unwelcome, yet felt unable to change. Many of the East Germans had serious difficulties in their marriages. Among the Russians, where family life was somewhat more traditional, half the respondents had been divorced and were now alone or in new marriages. I am not suggesting that absorption in work caused all the difficulties; housing, sexual incompatibility and different ideas about child rearing were problems for some of the people I spoke with. However, many of the men and women felt strong connections between absorption in work and the breaking up of their marriages. One East German, now having a fairly satisfactory second marriage, described the break-up of his first marriage.

> I left the house at six a.m. and usually had at least twelve hours with practically no free time – and then at night, I had to correct papers. My first wife worked for a television station. She . . . travelled a lot where there were outdoor programmes in certain villages and televised them on the spot. . . . We were absorbed into different problems and different worlds. Also, I did not have extreme sexual needs. . . . My wife began an affair with———, the man she worked with. Everyone thought they were married because she was always there, preparing everything, keeping everyone at a distance, afterwards celebrating together. I was absorbed in my own work and didn't notice anything. Once my wife called me and said something was happening, which I dismissed – and then later she said she had another man and wanted a divorce. I wouldn't have divorced her because of it. I thought after a while she would get over it but she wanted the divorce.

Here, according to the husband, the sexual incompatibility and the days away from each other caused the break-up of their marriage. Where the husbands and wives are separated from each other for longer periods of time, the absorptions in different worlds are even more intense.

> I married when I started university; my husband also studied. Two years later we had a child. Because he was such a brilliant student my husband began to travel to other countries as a representative of student associations. Less and less we shared the same world. He was involved in his problems, I was in mine, my studies and keeping the house, caring for the child. At the age of five or six months I could keep the child in a nursery until

I came home at one or two and then took him home. . . . After our studies, we divorced.

Each work world calls forth its own spirit; where these are seen as radically different, husbands and wives see the development of their *beings* moving in opposite directions. Sometimes they seek out a new partner who they hope will be more compatible; sometimes they resign themselves to living alone with their interests in order to keep the family together.

My husband is head of a department in a company. He claims he does too much administrative work, that there are arguments, that all the women talk about are clothes, etc. . . . but although he complains, he still keeps his job. He could refuse to do it, say he doesn't like it and get another one. We have less and less to talk about; the university is another world. We used to spend all our time together. . . . He says he believes the same way I do but he doesn't live that way. I met someone who took a job in———. He just took this as a job but at home he writes or paints, he swims, he walks in the woods. He knows how to live. I am thinking of separating.

We have different interests; I'm not interested in economics but in everything connected with the arts. He's not. He's not interested in my problems at school. He doesn't want professional problems brought into the household. I see he's down sometimes and would like to talk to him about it. Several days later, he might mention it. I go to art exhibitions alone. He watches television. I like talking and visiting and listening to music together. I like to speak about problems at work. . . . I thought it would be different, eating together and sharing our day together.

We always had different interests. I had no illusions when we married.

The man who said that a personal life alone without making a contribution would be boring added the following: 'I would like a wife who would share my interests, who would work with me but the chances of finding such a partner are small.' And at another time we were together:

I guess every man is looking for some combination of Simone de Beauvoir and Marilyn Monroe. If I had the ideal partner I wouldn't keep searching but I keep searching. You [to his wife] don't know anything about————. You're not interested in my work. When we work together late at night and sit down with some wine, if I discuss some problem she says it bores her.

Wife: One can't always talk about the same thing.

Absorption in work can also be an escape if life at home becomes too difficult. 'Often when things aren't good in our family, I don't want to bother with them. I want to do my work.'

Although more than half of the respondents thought the people they were closest to were their husbands or wives, several mentioned that their real friends were their colleagues at work.

I talk to a colleague, a very good friend of mine who lives near me.

My real friends are those I can talk to about my art, my work.

My closest friends are those I did my doctorate with. I can rely on them as I can on myself – more than my wife. I know of a case where a jealous woman reported that her husband was involved in suspicious activities and they all had to leave Moscow.

Being friendly with colleagues or involved in a work collective does not always mean that the married partner is excluded; actually, husbands and wives are encouraged to share in these activities together. There are problems, however. The partners may feel themselves excluded from the work collective. A sociologist suggested that in his department that was indeed the case. 'We have parties and common cultural outings. The wives and husbands are invited but what often happens is that the men get together to discuss work and the others don't know what to talk about and feel left out.' What can easily develop is a dislike for the partner's colleagues. Interestingly, it was the men, especially, who looked down on the friends of their wives.

He often criticized the friends I brought home so now I have a few I see without him.

My husband doesn't respect my friends. He says they really can't do anything – that's why they do the work they do.

Many of the husbands and wives enjoy leisure time activities together; however, these activities are a small part of their week. I was not sure if they were sufficient to counteract the strains and tensions of the couples who for the rest of the week were involved in different time- and energy-draining activities and who were having trouble because of it. In the Soviet Union, where the traditional family was stronger and great care and attention were given to the children, there was more of a counterbalancing force.

Those people who were in similar fields, medicine or the arts, or who were interested in and knew something about their partner's profession, seemed to be getting along better, as in American dual-career marriages.

The person I talk to is my wife. She is my friend. (Both husband and wife are educators)

I don't discuss problems with close friends – only in the house. (Both husband and wife are physicians)

After a while, we were both intensively involved in our work. Because my husband travelled often, we eventually decided to put our children in a boarding school and take them out for weekends. Our work, our revolutionary work, our discussions, our building up of a new society was the content of our lives. Through our work we made many friends, we had many gatherings and were intensely involved with our children, from the beginning trying to bring them up with a collective orientation. . . . Our work was the content of our lives. . . . With further industrialization of society, especially for scientists, the pressure became extraordinarily great – keeping up with what's done, administrative meetings and party meetings. (Both had been party workers)

What is new in advanced industrialized societies and finds particular support in socialist countries is the possibility for the woman to have separate and absorbing interests, to not depend on the marriage for the content of her life. The freeing of the woman to work has given her the possibilities and problems of being absorbed into another world and the freedom to get involved with other partners.

The new freedom of women, more generally of marriage partners from each other, may exert pressure on the marriage. Early communist theorists assumed that if both men and women worked, they would be able to marry for love and not for economic reasons and there would be more equality within the family. Some Western sociologists feared, however, that full employment of women and their involvement in affairs outside the community would lead to competition between husbands and wives. In the Soviet Union and in the German Democratic Republic, there is a realization that women's working may add to time pressures in the marriage; they do not automatically lead to equality. There is open discussion now about these issues. Rather than competition between husbands and wives, the problems seem much more to be work involvement and time.

It is possible to further clarify the implications of the emancipation of women for family life. Professional women, especially the East Germans, do not all accept marriage as a part of the good life. They are more freed from the feeling that marriage is necessary than professional women in the United States; they find it more emotionally and practically possible to live, and have children, outside of marriage than most American professional women.

About 10 per cent of the women students at our university have a child without marrying. They get used to living independently and may not marry – or they may not marry for a long time. (Estimation of an East German sociologist)

My daughter is pregnant but doesn't like the man and won't marry him. Many young people are like that, especially in this apartment house. I don't know what's the matter with them. In a smaller town, it wouldn't work.

How do the achievements of socialism and emancipation relate to such decisions not to marry? Because the woman has good child care and a job, she is not so dependent on the man. I had the impression, which was confirmed by an East German sociologist, that especially if the woman has been hurt, she may wait a long time to marry.

At twenty-four, I had my first relationship. We were together two or three times and then he left for the West without telling me. I waited one and a half years to hear from him but he never wrote. When that happened again, with another man, I began to mistrust men and think that's the way it is. I wasn't immoral but it didn't matter to me. I didn't understand why no one took me seriously enough to marry. My great love and the father of my son was married but in the end he chose to stay with his comfort. . . . I was very happy at thirty to have a child and felt I didn't need men any more . . . I didn't think of marrying. I could go to the theatre alone.

This particular woman, who is now married with two children, said she was thinking of leaving her present husband. 'I've thought of separating. I'm respected for my work; I'm emancipated. I've been in the same school for years and I have good contacts but I don't have the strength to start a big battle.'

For other women, marriage is seen as perhaps interfering with the rest of their lives; they are ambivalent about it. Again, this is especially true for some of the East Germans I spoke with.

I had a child with————. I brought her up alone although the father still has contact with us and is often here on visits. I was a student when we met and I wasn't ready to marry. I was absorbed in my work and hadn't all that time for him. Now I live with a man,————. I was used to coming home in the evening and doing what I wanted. Now there is pressure to talk, yet we are both so tired after work. Perhaps it will be easier in our new apartment. . . . On the other hand, it is good to be able to talk about problems at home.

I now live with————but he works somewhere else and we are only together at weekends. I'm trying to get him a position here but I don't know why one should marry. I'm not sure whether it's better to live together or see each other for weekends. I come home so tired I don't have the strength to talk. (Divorced woman with a child)

The questioning of marriage and the desire for equality with men, as I said before, were more prevalent among the East Germans than the Russians. One Soviet professional woman thought that men did not really want equality and so perhaps it was not such a good idea. Although I heard similar comments several times, in this case I suspected she was influenced even more in this direction by her new Israeli milieu and lack of professional opportunity. 'I now have the feeling that the husband has to be something higher. The wife has to keep the house in order. Especially as the man gets older, he wants the wife in the house.' Another Soviet woman actually thought equality harmful for the marital relationship.

> If a woman has an equal salary to the man's, she's not dependent. She can leave any time. . . . In some ways it's easier not to be married. It is natural for a woman to be somewhat dependent on a man. We, in the Soviet Union, *have* Women's Lib. Look where it got us.

These views were shared by only one East German woman I spoke to, a seventy-year-old widow I met in a restaurant: 'Do you know why we have a high divorce rate? The woman works and is exhausted. She has no energy left for anything, including love. She demands that the man help her. That goes against the natural authority of the male.'

The fact is that the East German woman, especially, does emphasize her independence. Several of the East German women I spoke with have their own bedrooms. They demand help, they demand time to improve their qualifications, they demand contributions to the care of the children and the household. There is often fighting; if the husband cannot accept these changes in the marriage, the consequences may be severe.

> Something has to be done in the house; if the husband is busy and the wife is busy, who will care for the children? Often the husband and wife both want to improve their qualifications and many of the husbands have traditional attitudes in the family. If he doesn't help her, she may leave the marriage. This is a transitional stage and there are many conflicts.

> The orientation of the man is completely old-fashioned; he believes he will set the tone for the household but the wife will not accept that any more.

These attitudes change slowly indeed; they are deeply rooted in the personality structure and go back to early childhood. Thus even couples who intend to lead their lives on a basis of equality find themselves ambivalent, strike compromises and get stuck in half-way arrangements.
In a few cases, there was complete sharing of household tasks:

> Look at our lampshades that we made. He made many things in the kitchen. He helps, cooks, exactly as I do. There is no other way. I am exactly equal, my work is exactly as important. (Woman professional who lives together with her friend at weekends)

The man may react by accusing the woman of doing too much outside the home.

> Sometimes my wife neglected everything because she was so intensely interested in her work.

> My husband watches television at night; I work. He would like me to be with him but for what? He just sits and watches television. He says that I do more than necessary.

> My husband accused me of not being interested in the house and exaggerating my work. He comes home, watches television and then goes to sleep – so that it doesn't matter if I work.

There were two dramatic cases where the wives expected help because they wanted to return to university and improve their qualifications. The first involved a woman who developed heart trouble and had to stay at home for some months.

> I counted on him to help me but he told me to leave if I didn't feel happy and that there was no reason why I should work. He began to see someone else and sometimes he was away nights. It lasted two years but I only found out the last half year. The woman wanted him to divorce me but he had no intention of doing so. . . . I said that I would work only half a day. . . . I was offered the job of being head of——[a prestigious international organization] in my area. It would have been fantastic but I would have had to work full-time and go to meetings at night. The young woman who eventually took the job had a husband who helped her in all ways.

In another family, the man I spoke with was still overwhelmed by the sequence of events in his marriage.

> I went away for a year to the Soviet Union. . . . My wife said that now she wanted to improve her qualifications, that I should do for her what she did for me. It was my hardest year at work. All sorts of commitments came due; it was not only the students but teaching and we had set a time for the completion of our team research. We used to go to concerts, theatre – now I was doing nothing but working. She couldn't get emotional attention from me and turned to someone in her school. We got a divorce and decided I would take care of the children because she's more nervous and gets easily excited.
>
> But what happened was that she remained in the apartment (getting new housing is difficult). I did the housework and took care of the children although she helped a bit. This weekend, for example, she was away. The relationship to the new man didn't work out. All her grounds for the divorce disappeared. I was doing the work and caring for the children. In addition, my work eased up, which she didn't believe would happen, so now she says she would like to continue living with me. I would have never expected all this. I didn't think it was so bad until it all happened.

Especially those wives whose husbands had more flexible and self-determined schedules felt their husbands could contribute more to the household than they did; they were also extremely jealous of their freer life style. The following conversation took place between a husband who had just come back from a weekend in Warsaw and his wife:

> Husband: 'The second night I returned to her house [the woman in Warsaw is a friend of his wife] she was in bed naked with her boyfriend and invited me into the room; together we drank as if it were the most natural thing to do.'

> Wife (furious at his enthusiasm): 'Every woman is more interesting than I am . . . I am so tired at night. I have to get up at six in the morning. He can regulate his own schedule.'

Another woman who taught adolescents had a husband at the university with a more flexible schedule. She complained that her husband did not do enough at home.

> I do more in the household than he does, housework and the education of the children. He can sleep late if he wants to. . . . On Sunday I'm already nervous. We have to plan everything in advance, for example, going to the theatre, because then I have to make up the work.

There were a few families where the husbands actually had the main burden of caring for the children and the household. The men had the more flexible schedules; they were musicians while their wives in some cases had more scheduled work. Sometimes, both the husbands and wives found the switching difficult. Complaints about the quality of the upbringing of the children and the difficulties for the man were minor, however, compared to the catastrophe which, according to my respondents, took place when the wife thought her work or her talent to be more important than her husband's obligations and refused to pay much attention either to the household or to the children. Although such attitudes on the part of men are no surprise to most women who until recently took for granted husbands who did not tune in extensively to the life of the family, women who show no great interest in the family are seen as shocking and unnatural by their husbands. In the first case, a violinist now divorced described his marriage to a ballerina.

> The profession itself interested her. . . . We had no private life. We didn't go out. I liked to walk in the woods of Moscow. My parents had a little datcha outside Moscow. These are very romantic things. All her energy went in her work. For her, the work came first. She didn't want children; I was more involved with our son than she was. . . . My parents were warm. 'Come,' they said, but there was never time.

An even more extreme situation developed in the first marriage of a composer to a pianist.

> While I was studying, I married a woman who wanted to be a

pianist and we had a child. She didn't want to do any work in the house. She had the idea that she was great, that she would be a great pianist and that I was much less in comparison. She couldn't cook or clean or do anything in the house. I did everything.

Problems of sharing in household tasks become public issues where there is no longer a 'fall back' person available, such as a grandmother, maid or unemployed wife. Although women continue to carry more than their half, so to speak, they are increasingly emancipated, capable and desirous of leading independent lives, much more than their Western counterparts. It is unlikely that this trend will reverse itself; family problems related to work are being considered now within a new context. The stage is set, the props are there; old milieus are unlikely to be recreated.

What does that mean as far as family and friendship relations are concerned? It is quite clear that both men and women want to find partners to share their lives with. Most people came from broken families or had parents who had died in the Second World War or who had spent many years in camps in the Soviet Union. This generation now has the material possibilities of establishing themselves in comfortable family settings and of having more of a sense of continuity in their own lives. Political uncertainty, on the one hand, adds to feelings of unease and insecurity which cause tensions in the family and, at the same time, increase a commitment and dependence on family members and friends one can trust. Work pressures, time pressures, commitment to one's professional life lead to escapist and retreatist tendencies outside work, concentration on one's private life, one's own family, own apartment and car, one's own vacation space. Everyday living within the family, however, is so burdened that the flow of work and family, public and private life become incompatible and unmanageable. Work, not as alienated labour but as a source of one's identification, as a focus for one's energies, professional, societal and emotional, is a joy and a burden in itself, just as the family is – an equally important centre of one's life. The manoeuvrability, the easiness of incorporating two such important aspects of one's being is limited; at least now, expectations of their being harmonious are unrealizable for most people.

Appendix

Notes on the Eastern European interviews
I spoke with Soviet Jews in Israel, in West Berlin and in the United States, concentrating primarily on their work and family lives before they left the USSR. In addition, I talked to East German professional men and women about work and family issues. I interviewed twenty professionals from the Soviet Union and thirteen professionals in the German Democratic Republic; in addition, three years later I interviewed a dozen more women, in the German Democratic Republic focusing on the work collective of academics; these were part of a separate study and therefore not listed in the tables. The Soviet immigrants in Israel and the United States had been in their new country from one to three years; the Soviet immigrants I spoke to in West Berlin had been in Germany from nine months to three years. All had been professionally trained in the Soviet Union and spent their working lives in the Soviet Union until they had emigrated. Both the emigrants and the citizens of the German Democratic Republic were in dual-career families.

These interviews took at least two hours each, but often the talks reflected only a part of my relationship with the respondents. Many of the Soviet Jews, unused to the limited nature of interviewing that American sociologists take for granted, had an expectation of a more continuing personal relationship the moment they agreed to the interview, which they usually did because of personal contact to someone we both knew in common. That meant in some cases there was visiting back and forth after the interview or eating out together; in one case in West Berlin, I attended the funeral of a man I interviewed and subsequently spent quite a bit of time with the family before I left the country. Often, the emigrants had many questions about the country they had just moved into or the country they expected to go to; they hoped I could help them with information and advice. This allowed me to know them in more than the interview setting which luckily enough was usually in the home or at work.

I also was in contact with some of the people who worked with the Soviet immigrants when they first arrived. In Israel, I spoke with a teacher who taught English to Russian professionals. These talks, in addition to the many voluntary observations on the Russian immigrants that Israelis were only too ready to make, helped shape my impressions of what I was seeing and hearing, though many of these remarks were rather stereotypical.

In West Berlin, it proved fairly difficult to get contacts. I knew the Rabbi of Berlin who spoke to me about his impressions of what the new immigrants were experiencing. A German Jewish graduate student at the university introduced me to a Russian family. Generally, the Jewish community representatives, however, as well as the Soviet Jews I met in Berlin, were hesitant and not enthusiastic about the interviews. I had a formal and predictable talk with the manager of the refugee camp many of the Russians come to before moving to private apartments, and with a German teacher with whom many Russians studied at the Goethe Institute. The teacher, who had spent many hours with the Russian immigrants, was very helpful to talk to.

While, for a foreigner, it is not illegal to talk extensively with people in East Berlin without special permission, I sought to receive formal authorization for an interview study because this would allay fears of East Germans I intended to speak with concerning my role and identity; no Western sociologist has received such authorization before. I spent weeks trying to get authorization, learning to know people who were sympathetic to what I was trying to do, phoning endless times only to have to phone back again, and hours travelling back and forth and at the border. For a long time I did not succeed in getting such authorization; at the end of my stay I did, but the officials of the institution were not able to help me with contacts. I decided to have informal talks with people rather than do formal interviews.

In the German Democratic Republic, too, the actual talks were only a small part of my contacts. I became very close to the people who helped me find respondents. We saw each other frequently, at their apartments, at restaurants and the theatre. Nearly all the respondents wanted to meet me before consenting to a talk; in these cases I made special trips to meet the people and returned once more to speak extensively with them. Most of these initial meetings which people requested before they consented to our talk took place in the apartment of the people who had introduced us. I also slowly learned to know a few of the people I talked with and their husbands and wives. These experiences were intense, probably because of the peculiar nature of our relationship but also because of the limited time period we knew we had.

I made notes after returning to West Berlin. I thought

remembering conversations would be problematical, but to my surprise, my memory proved strong enough and the interview notes were fuller and more encompassing than with the Russian Jews. I think in part that was due to being able to walk the streets, eat in the restaurants and cafés, wander through bookstores, walk past the same river with swans, the same bombed-out churches, the same Baroque buildings as the people I talked with did, so I was able to get more of a sense of all the intangible smells and moods than I could with the Russians I spoke with, who had left their homes, despite the many good and intense talks we had. Equally important was the problem of following an interview guide more closely and taking notes for such personal topics with the Soviet Jews. In the Notes on Interviewing of my first set of interviews, I talked about friendship and conversation involving an exchange of confidence. Using the interview guide the interviewer is seeking responses to specific questions. Even when conversational exchanges are made, the very presence of an interview guide creates an unusual atmosphere.

An accidental encounter at the border brought me into contact with a German Jewish woman living in East Berlin who had taught at a university in the Soviet Union. She spontaneously added some of her impressions to mine about university teaching and personal relationships both in the Soviet Union and in East Berlin. I also had the opportunity to have a long talk with two sociologists at the Humboldt University. With one, I was able to have a long, open and personal conversation about pressures at work and their effects on his marriage.

As a sociologist going into an unfamiliar culture and having to speak with officials and professional men and women I could not help but reflect on my understanding of the conversations we had. Two powerful examples come to mind: the first is the extensive use of the philosophical language of historical and dialectical Marxism among intellectuals; the second is the communication with bureaucrats in the German Democratic Republic whose power was strong, and, at the same time, on occasion not quite clear either to themselves or to the people with whom they speak. These experiences gave me an intense reminder of glimpses I had before in 'normal conversations' about the problematic nature of communication. What does it mean when people talk to each other or does the conversation have meanings which are connected only in a tenuous way to what is actually being said? How does one reach workable understandings when words stray so far from their traditional, taken-for-granted meanings? Or how does one adjust in an unfamiliar society to new expectations of heightened sensitivities in conversations so that one becomes aware of intense meanings in casual suggestions, questions or doubts? My contacts among the East German professionals were sufficiently varied so that I could overcome some of these barriers to understanding; by the time I left I felt more familiar and comfortable with the language codes.

One also must remember that for the most part the conversations took place in a day of one person's life. That person came to the interview from somewhere and left the interview for somewhere. Our talk was a glimpse of feelings and reactions of a specific time. An analysis of the responses as I do now, reviewing my notes jotted down after the interview, finalizes, too strongly sets boundaries on what is really happening to the people I spoke with. Giving each of them a chapter and letting them tell their own stories would provide a deeper understanding of their individual lives even though the contingencies of a single day's experience would not be eliminated. I felt, however, I had to take apart and put together social patterns that seemed to emerge from the individual stories rather than be a recorder of tales; such a synthesizing analysis that we sociologists engage in is a necessary and dubious enterprise at the same time.

Since I was dependent on personal contacts for interviews, I could not easily determine the composition of my sample with regard to age, different career stages or participation and non-participation in bureaucracies. The age range of the East Berlin respondents is much narrower than the sample of Russian Jews; fortunately, they were at different points in their careers so that I could get a sense of what changed or remained the same for them during these years.

In Table 4.4 the professions of the respondents in the Soviet Union as well as in their new countries are listed. All of the respondents in Israel were working except for one woman physician who had decided to take time out to learn Hebrew. However, not everyone was doing the same work they did in the Soviet Union. The translator and industrial engineer had different jobs is Israel. The medical doctor who was head of a department in the Soviet Union was working as an 'ordinary' doctor now. That was also true for the doctor who had

TABLE 4.4 *Professions of Soviet respondents at home and in their new country*

Soviet Union	United States	Israel	Germany
Males			
Dentist			(Died)
Engineer			Clerk
Industrial engineer			Researcher in a university institute
Pianist		Pianist	
Physician	Physician		
Physician		Physician	
Technical engineer			Unemployed
Physicist			Unemployed
Psychiatrist		Psychiatrist	
Psychiatrist		Psychiatrist	
Psychiatrist		Psychiatrist	
Violinist	Violinist		
Violinist			Violinist
Females			
Anthropologist	Unemployed		
Industrial engineer		Tax inspector	
Fashion designer			Unemployed
Translator		Saleswoman in a bookstore	
High school teacher			Unemployed
High school teacher			Lecturer at a university
Physician		Unemployed	

immigrated to the United States. Several of the Russian women who immigrated to West Berlin were not working. In part that was due to having the financial possibility to wait until the proper job was found because of support given by the German government. Those men who had not yet found jobs in Germany had only arrived in the last few months.

5 Conclusion: Professional work and personal life in capitalist and socialist societies

I have attempted to explore the effects of work demands on family and friendship relationships. The question is crucial to the quality of living in any modern society. Its importance was recognized as early as in the work of the young Marx: alienation which, in its extreme forms, results from the organization of the capitalist mode of production, destroys the human qualities of man and thus the possibility for meaningful social relations outside work.[1] A second important condition contributing to a humanly fulfilled relationship between marriage partners is, at least in modern society, a fundamental equality. Here again, Marxists and other social thinkers of the nineteenth century not only recognized the importance of equality in marriage but understood how sexual equality and inequality are rooted in the organization of work and the conditions of production.

In an exploratory study of middle-class married adults, one or both of whom work in professional occupations, I looked at the effects work pressures have on personal relations outside of work in the United States and in two European socialist countries – the USSR and the German Democratic Republic. A major initial hypothesis was that the marital relationship would be affected very differently by work pressures if the wife worked pro-fessionally outside the household than if she stayed at home. Comparison of single- and dual-career families was therefore important in my analysis of different relations between work and marital roles in the United States. In addition, dual-career families are the norm in European socialist societies, while they have become more common in the United States only in recent years. Thus the contrast between the two marriage types is closely related to the second basic comparison of this study, the comparison of socialism and capitalism as different socio-economic contexts shaping the effects of work pressures on human relations outside of work. I compared dual-career families in the United States with those in the Soviet Union and the German Democratic Republic in order to determine whether, firstly, the socialist societies succeeded to a greater degree in reducing the alienation of professionals at work and, secondly, whether there was any carry-over from such differences in employment and work into the marital, as well as the friendship relations outside work. Since there has been little research on these problems, I did an exploratory study based on intensive interviews with a limited number of people. I focused on the interrelationships, the links between work and family as well as between work and friendship relations. My goal was to develop hypotheses rather than test them. My conclusions are thus tentative and in need of further investigation.

Living in a single-career family has definite effects on the marital relationship.[2] The wife tends to develop an ambivalent attitude towards her husband's career. On the one hand, she resents the time and attention he gives to his work; on the other hand, she has ambitions for his career development which may or may not be realistic and which may prohibit him from having what she would consider an adequate involvement in the family and in the marriage. While the wife is often lonely and depressed, the husband tends not to fully perceive the intensity of her deprivation. Just as she is not able to completely understand her husband's world and work involvement, he focuses on her activities outside the house and is frequently insensitive to her life in the family.

Increasingly, she accepts the responsibility and control of the house;[3] her husband takes for granted her involvement in it. After several years, the woman believes she cannot easily give up the management of the house and work outside. Who would take care of everything? Her husband, on the other hand, is not ready to increase his already heavy work load to seriously share the household responsibilities. Most of the men I spoke to thought their wives might return to work after the children were older. Such a delayed return meant they would not be burdened by many increased responsibilities. They would also be relieved of the worry of providing their wives the time and attention the women said they needed. The longer these women stay outside their work, however, the more difficult it is for them psychologically and professionally to return.

Nearly all the women in the United States and in Eastern Europe I spoke with married with some expectation of fulfilling traditional female roles. The range of expectation, of course, varied according to their past education, the vision they had of their future work years, and the social and economic supports and public discussion of the new role of women. In the single-career families, women questioned their traditional roles because of their feelings of loneliness and isolation, of having the burden of the family without many of the emotional rewards. In dual-career families, in both the United States and in Eastern Europe, an increasing commitment to their careers and a rejection of their traditional roles evolved after the women spent time working in their professions.

In dual-career families, both husbands and wives have a better understanding both of the world of work and the tasks and problems at home. This is particularly true if the couple envisioned a dual-career involvement from the beginning – having attended professional school at the same time or having met as professionals. Members of dual-career families tend to be more sensitive and realistic about work pressures and possibilities and, at the same time, share household responsibilities. Although the husband is still deeply concerned about the progress of his career, he tends to be somewhat less consumed by ambition compared to his counterpart in the single-career family; this is due to his family commitment and to the difficulties in simply shifting responsibility to his wife as work involvement increases.

The women in dual-career families receive more respect from their husbands than those in single-career families and tend to respect themselves more than women who do not work outside the household. They are less overwhelmed by their husbands' successes and failures and have less of a feeling of being controlled by forces they can neither fully understand nor affect.

While the relationship between husband and wife in dual-career families is based more often on equality, mutual understanding and accommodation, there is a tendency for husbands and wives to lead independent, parallel lives with less time and energy available for common and shared experiences than is felt desirable. Furthermore, the motto, 'You do your thing, I'll do mine', is part of the marriage credo of many young American couples. There is a concentration on individual success and personal fulfilment which is very much part of the economic and political milieu in which they have been raised. In addition to the past subordination of the woman's needs to her husband's goals, the outer and inner pressures to continually strive to improve one's position necessarily militate against a principal commitment to more collective goals.

In Eastern Europe, especially in the German Democratic Republic, the men and women I spoke with showed an intense preoccupation with what was happening outside their family, not only to their lives as individuals and professionals but to their lives as politically responsible members of their society. There was political discussion between partners, even fundamental disagreements. They worried about politics; in a few cases, they expressed fear about political developments. The different ideological and cultural context in Eastern Europe makes the American kind of individualism less legitimate. Both men and women are educated at an early age to be responsible and giving to others at school, at work, and in the home as well. These ideals are related to the question of what 'real' emancipation is. Western emancipation is largely, although not completely, individualistic and thus tends to define the solidarity of the couple as a lack of emancipation. Commitment to the family in this view reduces the ability of the husband and wife to fulfil themselves as individuals.

Those husbands and wives who share common professional interests seem more able to tune in to their spouses' problems and concerns and feel less of a separation in their lives as a couple than the men and women who are in completely different fields.

Changes toward new, more egalitarian roles of husband and wife in dual-career families are less than complete. Especially when there are children, there remains an asymmetry of family roles in nearly all dual-career families. This may be understood as a persistence of traditional sex roles which give the wife primary responsibility for the children and housework and induce in her a stronger commitment and concern with personal relations and openness with her husband. This continuation of traditional sex roles is not only a matter of deeply rooted individual attitudes, expectations and conceptions of self and others; it is reinforced or weakened to the extent in which women's work outside the house is accepted and expected in society as well as supported and institutionalized. Two aspects are worth emphasizing. Firstly, if professional work of middle-class women is, as in the United States, regarded as voluntary and optional, both society and the individual continue to see the husband as the main breadwinner and as less able than his wife to deviate from the institutional expectations of his work organization. Conversely, women for the same reasons develop ambivalent feelings, complicated by guilt and compensating insistence, about their work, their children and their family life.

Secondly, in addition to attitudes – of the people immediately involved as well as of people in their social environment and in society at large – specific supports for working wives and mothers make an important difference for the development of a new division of labour in dual-career families and for the quality of the personal relationships between husband and wife in these families. This assertion derives both from comparing those American families who had full-time help or household arrangements that went beyond their immediate family, with other dual-career families in this country and from comparing the overall situation in the United States with the much more developed supports for the working wife and mother in the socialist countries.

In the Eastern European socialist societies, women's employment is not only accepted but expected and firmly institutionalized, i.e., legitimated by dominant values and beliefs as well as supported by various arrangements that provide practical help. As a consequence, the vast majority of families in these socialist societies are dual-career families. That does not mean socialist societies have solved the 'women's problem'. The participation of women in the work force does not insure their equality in the family. Cultural traditions, for example, continue to have impact on the relationship. If we look at the differences which seem to exist between the East German men and women and those from the Soviet Union with respect to these problems[4], despite an acceptance by the husbands of their wives' right to work and some sharing of family responsibilities, there were greater problems with the participation of men in household work in some of the Russian families. A few thought they should not be asked to take over the traditional work of the household. My East German respondents, younger and more integrated into the political system of their country, reported fewer problems in this regard than the Jewish emigrants from the Soviet Union, although there was no difference in the high proportion of women working. Furthermore, it cannot be taken for granted that socialist policy will necessarily favour the advancement of women in equal work participation. If women are no longer needed in the work force or if it is decided to take drastic measures to increase the birth rate and further emphasize the importance of the family as a socializing agent, incentives may be provided to keep women at home with their children for a long period of time.[5] As welcome as these incentives are for some women, professionals may have difficulties reintegrating themselves in their work organizations after a long period at home. In the immediate future, I see this as an unlikely development in the Soviet Union and the German Democratic Republic because of the continuing need for women's labour and at least some public expression of the potential danger of any policy encouraging a return of the woman to her traditional roles of housewife and mother. Thus far, the stronger institutionalization of women's work outside the household and the rapid decline of the traditional single-career family as an institutional pattern is one major difference between capitalist and socialist societies which profoundly affects the impact of professional work on personal relations in marriage.

The women I spoke to from socialist societies would not consider remaining at home and giving up their participation in the world of work. At the same time, especially in the German Democratic Republic, they expect their husbands to share equally with them in the household and tell them so; after all, their work demands are as important as those of their husbands. Many of the men I spoke to responded to these demands. If not, their marriage was in danger of breaking up.[6]

Generally, the institutional and ideological supports given to women, especially in the German Democratic Republic, facilitate their independence. The professional women I spoke to did not take for granted that they had to marry. Sociologists estimated that 10 per cent of the women studying at the university decide to have children without marrying. If the woman chooses to divorce or not to marry, she is not isolated. She has her work, she has her colleague group. She has access to *Cribbes* for her child; she has the right to an apartment. The stability of the marriage, then, is not based on the economic dependence of the woman. That women are no longer economically dependent on their husbands, however, does not mean they all have an interest in abandoning their families. On the contrary, both in the Soviet Union and the German Democratic Republic, there was a great commitment among many of the men and women I spoke with to retaining the family and participating in a common, shared life.

A major initial hypothesis regarding differences between socialist and capitalist societies which guided my research was that reduced competition and more generally less alienation among professional workers in socialist societies would improve the chances of humane, intense and open personal relations outside work. It appears indeed that East European professionals are less alienated at work than their American counterparts. While both are deeply involved in the professional aspects of their work, professionals in the East European countries feel more secure in their positions than many American professionals; they experience less disparity in salary, and their projects are often co-operative. Those Eastern European professionals who identify with the political goals of the state see their work and their professional expertise as a contribution to their society and believe they can sometimes influence policy. I tried to establish links between these aspects of decreased alienation at work and a more relaxed atmosphere at home, an atmosphere that encouraged mutual respect between husband and wife and left more time and energy for openness and sensitivity with spouses and friends. I was better able to establish such links between decreased alienation at work and friendship relations than I was between decreased alienation and family relations.

It would be premature to abandon this hypothesis about the consequences of alienation at work on personal relations outside work altogether. However, I propose to qualify it with two other hypotheses, one concerning other pressures and problems which interfere with relaxed and humane family relations and do so more in the contemporary socialist societies of Eastern Europe than in the United States, and another about the character of professional work in both contemporary socialist and capitalist societies.

There are pressures and constraints of daily life unrelated to work which can have similar effects on personal relations outside of work as competitive work pressures and ambitions. Some of these seem more prevalent in the German Democratic Republic and the Soviet Union than in the United States. They include the lack of good and easily available housing accommodation for at least some of the professionals, the time and effort required for obtaining a variety of desirable consumer goods, and – for some at least – the strains of the political atmosphere. These and similar factors can counterbalance the effects of reduced competition and alienation as well as of the structural supports for working women as far as the quality of the marital relationship is concerned.

The second proposition qualifying the effects of different degrees of alienation at work pertains to the character of professional work. While it is more autonomous, more controlled by the practitioners and typically more meaningful than work in most other occupations, it also involves the practitioner more intensely and more personally. Both internalized work commitments and institutionally imposed expectations thus tend to be stronger. We may speak here of a paradox of professional work: the same factors that reduce alienation also increase personal involvement in one's work. This can have destructive effects on a rich personal and family life outside of work unless work commitments and institutional demands are well integrated with the needs and circumstances of family life.[7]

The more cooperative and secure work conditions in the socialist societies in Eastern Europe favour and encourage friendship relations. A work colleague group develops which is important both for the possibility of friendship at work and the carry-over of these friendships to one's personal life outside work. Work relationships are not interfered with by the kind of competition that exists among many professionals in capitalist society; furthermore, in a sometimes unpredictable political atmosphere, friends can be trusted to support and help you.

Friendships among men in the United States and among many professional women are not only restricted by involvement in work and the overload of family and work commitments but by the intense competition in many work situations. Those few professionals who were able to relieve feelings of competition at work by creating an atmosphere of co-operation in their smaller work group were highly aware of the destructive possibilities of a competitive environment. Most accepted competition, however, as a natural drive, rather than as a response shaped by culture and society. Especially as they got older, many of these men and women, although certainly not all, were aware and sorry not to have friends; they felt it as an intense loss in their lives. Although not all friendships are made among colleagues at work, sharing professional concerns and commitments is not unimportant to the friendship relation in a society where interests and commitments are rather specialized. Therefore the professional depends to some degree on his work organization for friendships and for the habits of interacting with others that are developed.

However, while this difference between capitalist and socialist society is important, the paradox of professional work affects friendship as well as marital relations. The supports given in socialist societies are only the beginnings of solutions. Reduced and flexible working hours for both men and women, increased sharing of tasks, and the open and sharp questioning of what is happening and what should happen in the work world of professionals may lead to a lessening of the tension between work and personal life. Dealing with this tension, intellectually and politically, remains an unfinished task.

This study has raised a number of issues which deserve much more reflection and discussion than they have received. The critical standard that underlies my investigation is a belief in the importance of deep personal relations based on stable commitments. This does not exclude work as an opportunity for human fulfilment but raises the critical question of whether certain forms of work organization and attitudes toward work endanger and undermine such human relationships. In pursuing this question, I have looked at different forms of marital relationships as well as different involvements in professional work in capitalist and in socialist societies. While I found important variations, the corroding effect on human relations was a problem in all the different patterns of life I studied, though varying significantly in degree.

My study dealt with the experiences of real people in three societies which differ in significant respects. I explored how men and women tried to deal with these problems in their personal and professional lives within a specific political and economic context. Recording, interpreting and reflecting on their efforts and their sense of alternatives and possibilities in their lives concerned me more than a utopian vision of new forms of social life. Both modes of inquiry can be seen as complementary. The utopian vision opens up new possibilities of action and thought. Yet, if it is not based on an understanding of real social structures and relationships, it remains utopian in the negative sense of the word, an illusion.

Notes

Chapter 1

1. These interviews were broken down in the following way: ten interviews with 'at-home' wives of professional men, ten interviews with professional men whose wives remained at home, ten interviews with wives working in their professions, ten interviews with husbands with wives working in their professions.
2. I decided first to interview some professional men and women in the United States, Israel and West Berlin, who had emigrated from the Soviet Union. Since I expected attitudes to the Soviet Union to be rather negative after immigration. I planned to interview people who had been in their new country for at least a year. I not only hoped for a more careful comparison of the different systems but since the immigrants would now know some English, Hebrew or German there was also the possibility of having more intensive conversations with them. Interviewing emigrants is problematical indeed because they are a biased population. I therefore decided to speak with professional men and women who lived in East Berlin, concentrating on the same issues as I did with the Soviets and Americans. The addition of citizens from the German Democratic Republic into my study, combined with the possibility of learning to know their environment more directly, proved extremely helpful for my understanding of the issues I was interested in.
3. Theodore Caplow has a long list of how professionals are expected to behave outside work (Caplow, 1954, p. 125).
4. For some interesting studies of the process of becoming a professional, see Lortie (1966, p. 98); Becker and Carper (1956); and Merton, Reader and Kendall (1957).
5. Goode (1960).
6. Role theory provides some useful clues here. See Merton (1957, pp. 281–6).
7. Agyris also discusses self-esteem (1964, pp. 26–8).
8. In 1977, nearly half of all women over sixteen were in the labour force (*Statistical Abstracts of the United States*, 1978). The proportion of women working in the twenty to twenty-four-year-old age group increased from 50 per cent in 1964 to 61 per cent in 1973. The percentage for the twenty-five to thirty-five-year-old group rose from 37 to 50 per cent, including 75 per cent of those women without children. In the twenty to twenty-four-year-old group, 86 per cent of women college graduates were employed as opposed to 71 per cent fourteen years earlier. But the fastest rise of all took place among women with young children. From 1959 to 1974, the employment rate for

180

mothers with children under three more than doubled, from 15 to 31 per cent, and that for mothers with children three to five years old increased from 25 to 39 per cent. Chafe (1976), p. 25.

9. The rate of divorce increased from 1.1 per thousand population in 1959 to 3.4 per thousand in 1976. For a technical analysis of the available data, see Anderson (1978).

10. As early as 1959, 49 per cent of all people who completed higher or university education were women (Goode, 1963, p. 62).

11. See also Lapidus (1978), and Jancar (1978); for Czechoslovakia, Scott (1974).

12. The initial revolutionary drive for greater equality was slowed and partly reversed during the rule of Stalin, but then resumed in moderate form under his successors. Engineering and technical workers, for instance, who in 1940 earned on the average slightly more than double the average salary of manual workers, in 1966 earned only 1.4 times as much as manual workers (Lane, 1971, p. 73). The role of political factors in shaping the distribution of material and immaterial privilege, as distinguished from the forces of supply and demand, is analysed by Goldthorpe (1966), Parkin (1971) as well as Lane (1971). See also Matthews (1972) and McAuley (1979) on socio-economic inequality in the Soviet Union.

Chapter 2

1. Two years after the interview with this woman, she told me they had separated.

2. Furthermore, two years after the interview with the wife of the instructor still in graduate school, she, too, informed me they had separated.

3. One might speculate that the reactions are in part shaped by the men's experiences with their mothers. These were varied, too. Table 2.5 shows that eight of the men had mothers who worked outside the house during their marriages; however, four of these women waited until their children were in high school or had graduated before working outside the house. Five of the eight women worked because it was financially necessary.

Chapter 3

1. Although I interviewed ten men and ten women, I have only seventeen families; in three of the families, I interviewed both husband and wife. On several issues, I gathered information both on the person interviewed and his or her spouse.

2. Charlotte Weissberg suggested that perhaps there is some self-selection of husbands who marry career women. Personality differences may be important; for example, a man may have enough ego strength to be able to live with a woman as successful as he is or a husband may be afraid of having the complete responsibility for the support of the family. Certain professional men may simply find career women more interesting. As I will

discuss later on, many feel able to share more of their lives with women who had concrete involvements in that world of work.

3. See, for example, Parsons (1954).

Chapter 4

1. For more details on these interviews, see the appendix to this chapter, 'Notes on the Eastern European interviews'.
2. This issue is also further discussed in the appendix, 'Notes on the Eastern European interviews'.
3. Jan Myrdal, in a personal conversation, believed that a definite and closed elite existed in the GDR: 'They marry within their class . . . they get special privileges. That was the only way they could keep the intellectuals there'.
4. Engels (1942, pp. 65–6).
5. Grant, Nigel (1979), p. 136.
6. Grant (1979, p. 15).
7. Grant (1979, p. 53).
8. Other people with extensive first-hand experience of the Soviet Union do, however, report widespread use of private tutors, especially on the part of students seeking entry to higher educational institutions.
9. Makarenko (1967), pp. xi–xii.
10. Grant (1979, p. 50).
11. Bronfenbrenner (1970, p. 56).
12. Ibid., pp. 52–3.
13. Grunert-Bronnen (1970), p. 29.
14. Bronfenbrenner (1970, pp. 53–4).
15. See for Poland, Sarapata (1974); Malewski (1974).
16. Bronfenbrenner (1970, p. 54).
17. 'The examinations are partly written, partly oral and are assessed on a five-point scale, from five (excellent) to one (poor)' (Grant 1979, p. 118). Students take examinations in four or five areas.
18. Grant (1979, pp. 135–6).
19. See Caplow (1954), Hall (1969) and Reiss (1955).
20. Here I exclude entrance into university; as I said before, many people were tense before acceptance.
21. Mark Field, during a personal conversation, said the problem of women doctors in the Soviet Union not wanting to spend time in rural areas was so great that the number of women accepted into medical school has been reduced.
22. Three years later, I returned to the German Democratic Republic and did a separate study on the work collective of academics. See Marilyn Rueschemeyer, 'Social and Work Relations of Professional Women: an Academic Collective in the German Democratic Republic', *East Central Europe*, Fall 1980.
23. Menschik and Leopold (1974, p. 23). For the Soviet Union, see Lapidus (1978), pp. 123–60.
24. This information came from Menschik and Leopold, *Ibid.*, p. 25 and Elsner (1979).

25. Mandel (1975), p. 319.
26. This remark was made by the son of a woman I interviewed and contradicted by the mother who said that her mother had to work.
27. Grunert-Bronnen (1970), postscript.
28. In my sample, there were fewer men than women in school to improve their qualifications although the opportunity is given to everyone.

Chapter 5

1. Among the different possible interpretations of Marx's concept, I have relied heavily on Blauner for specific formulations. See Chapter 1.
2. The propositions that follow state differences in frequency without always qualifying each sentence with clauses such as 'tend more', 'more often than', etc.
3. Kanter (1977 – *Men and Women of the Corporation*) described a similar response of wives of executives and professionals in the corporation she studied 'with the wife erecting an exclusionary barrier over her own technical domain of home and children and getting angry if the husband threatened her power there' (p. 114). Efforts to involve wives in the organization through an experimental educational unit for both husbands and wives were highly successful; however, this effort was not repeated again (p. 115). In addition, as just stated, all are hypothetical.
4. Here again, I am interested in developing hypotheses. I cannot with great assurance take for granted that the Russian professional emigrants were representative of their larger professional community.
5. See Lapidus (1978, p. 307) for a discussion of these incentives in Hungary and Scott (1974) on Czechoslovakia.
6. The exceptions in both the Soviet Union and in Eastern Germany included five families in which the wife expected the husband to take full responsibility for the children and the household so that she could devote herself completely to her career. The husband could not accept his wife's dropping out to such an extent from the family; among the people I spoke to, these marriages ended in divorce.
7. Lein *et al.*, (1974) in a study of working men and women argue that where there was sharing of the work at home on the basis of flexible work conditions, the fathers often enjoyed their new roles. Bailyn (1972) observes a valuing of family life by professionals in organizations. However, any assumption that individuals can simply decide to value their family lives and share equally at home underestimates the power and structural arrangements of the work organization. Bailyn found that men in management and technological fields who responded to family demands had difficulties at work; in the American context these problems adversely affected the self-images of the men. As Rapoport and Rapoport (1976, p. 327) rightly suggest, 'indications are that male responses in the humanistic or androgynous direction are still relatively marginal and visionary, with only a beginning of a men's movement to exert pressures on the social system beyond the personal situations of individual persons'.

Bibliography

Adams, Donald K. (ed.) (1966) *Introduction to Education: a Comparative Analysis* (Belmont, California: Wadsworth).

Agyris, Chris (1964) *Integrating the Individual and the Organization* (New York: Wiley).

Anderson, Barbara (1978) 'Changes in Marriage and Marital Dissolution in the Soviet Union, 1959–1976', Department of Sociology and Population Studies and Training Center, Brown University, Providence, Rhode Island.

Atkinson, Dorothy, Dallin, Alexander and Lapidus, Gail Warshofsky (eds) (1977) *Women in Russia* (Stanford University Press).

Bailyn, Lotte (1977) 'Involvement and Accommodation in Technical Careers: an Inquiry into the Relation to Work at Mid-Career', in John Van Maanen, *Organizational Careers* (New York: Wiley, 1977) pp. 109–32.

Bartolmè, Fernando (1974) 'Executives as Human Beings', in Joseph H. Pleck and Jack Sawyer (eds), *Men and Masculinity*, (New Jersey: Prentice-Hall, 1974) pp. 100–6.

Becker, Howard S. and Carper, James W. (1956) 'The Development of Identification with an Occupation', *American Journal of Sociology*, vol. 61, pp. 289–98.

Becker, Howard S. and Carper, James W. (1956) 'The Elements of Identification with an Occupation', *American Sociological Review*, vol. 21, pp. 341–7.

Bendix, Reinhard and Lipset, Seymour M. (1966) *Class, Status, and Power*, 2nd edn (New York: Free Press).

Blau, Peter M. and Duncan, Otis D. (1967) *The American Occupational Structure* (New York: Wiley).

Blauner, Robert (1964) *Alienation and Freedom* (University of Chicago Press).

Bowles, Samuel and Gintis, Herbert (1976) *Schooling in Capitalist America* (New York: Basic Books).

Bronfenbrenner, Urie (1970) *Two Worlds of Childhood: US and USSR* (New York: Basic Books).

Brown, Archie (1979) 'Eastern Europe: 1968, 1978, 1998', *Daedalus* (Winter) vol. 108, no. 1, pp. 151–74.

Brown, Archie and Gray, Jack (eds) (1977) *Political Culture and Political Change in Communist States* (London: Macmillan, and New York: Holmes and Meier).

Campbell, Angus, Converse, Philip and Rodgers, Willard L. (1976) *The Quality of American Life* (New York: Russell Sage Foundation).

Caplow, Theodore (1954) *The Sociology of Work* (Minneapolis: University of Minnesota Press).

Caplow, Theodore (1958) *The Academic Market Place* (New York: Basic Books).

Chafe, William H. (1976) 'Looking Backward in Order to Look Forwards, in Juanita M. Kreps (ed.), *Women and the American Economy* (Englewood Cliffs, New Jersey: Prentice Hall) pp. 6–30.

Clark, Robert A., Nye, F. Ivan and Gecas, Viktor (1978) 'Husband's Role Involvement and Marital Role Performance', *Journal of Marriage and the Family*, vol. 40, no. 1, pp. 9–21.

Coleman, James S. (1966) *Equality of Educational Opportunity*, (Washington, DC: US Dept. of Health, Education and Welfare, Office of Education, US Government Printing Office).

Curti, Merle E. (1935) *The Social Ideas of American Educators*, (New York: Charles Scribner).

Dalton, Melvin (1956) 'Informal Factors in Career Achievement', *American Journal of Sociology*, vol., 21 pp. 341–7.

Dewey, John (1940) *Education Today*, ed. by Joseph Ratner (New York: Putnam).

Dornberg, John (1968) *The Other Germany* (New York: Doubleday).

Dubin, Robert (1956) 'Industrial Workers' Worlds: a Study of the "Central Life Interests" of Industrial Workers', *Social Problems*, vol. 3 (January) pp. 131–42.

Duncan, Otis Dudley, Featherman, David L. and Duncan, Beverly (1972) *Socioeconomic Background and Achievement* (New York: Seminar Press).

Dunn, Stephen and Dunn, Ethel (1977) 'The Study of the Soviet Family in the USSR and in the West', *Slavic Studies Working Paper* 1 (Columbus, Ohio: American Association for the Advancement of Slavic Studies).

Elsner, Eva-Maria (1979) 'Probleme der Lebensweise und der Gesellschaftlichen Stellung der Frau im Sozialismus', *Wissenschaftliche Zeitschrift der Wilhelm-Pieck Universität Rostock*, vol. 28, Gesellschafts und Sprachwissenschaftliche Reihe, Heft 1/2.

Engels, Friedrich (1942) *The Origin of the Family, Private Property and the State*, Marxist Library, Works of Marxism–Leninism, vol. XXIII (New York: International Publishers).

Epstein, Cynthia Fuchs (1971) *Women's Place*, (Berkeley: University of California Press).

Epstein, Cynthia (1971) 'Law Partners and Marital Partners', *Human Relations*, vol. 24, no. 6, pp. 549–64.

Fisher, Charles S. (1973) 'Some social Characteristics of Mathematicians and their Work', *American Journal of Sociology*, vol. 78, no. 5 (March), pp. 1094–1118.

Fogarty, Michael R., Rapoport, Rhona and Robert (1971) *Sex, Career and Family* (London: Allen and Unwin for P.E.P.).

Editors of Fortune (1956) *The Executive Life* (New York: Doubleday).

Frank, Gerald (1949) *The Society as the Patient* (New Brunswick: Rutgers University Press).

Friedenberg, Edgar, Z. (1965) *The Dignity of Youth and Other Atavisms* (Boston: Beacon Press).

Friedmann, George (1961) *The Anatomy of Work* (New York: Free Press of Glencoe).

Fromm, Erich (1962) 'Personality and the Market Place', in Sigmund Nosow and William H. Form, (eds). *Man, Work, and Society* (New York: Basic Books).

Geiger, Kent (1965) 'The Soviet Family', in M.F. Nimkoff (ed.), *Comparative Family Systems* (Boston: Houghton Mifflin), pp. 301–28.

Glenn, Norval D., Alston, Jon P. and Weiner, David (1970), *Social Stratification: A Research Bibliography* (Berkeley, California: Glendessary Press).

Goldthorpe, J. H. (1966) 'Social Stratification in Industrial Society', in Bendix and Lipset, *Class, Status and Power*, 2nd edn. (New York: Free Press), pp. 648–59.

Goode, William J. (1960) 'Norm Commitment and Conformity to Role-Status Obligations', *American Journal of Sociology*, vol. 66 (November) pp. 246–48.

Goode, William J. (1963) *World Revolutions and Family Patterns* (New York: The Free Press of Glencoe).

Goode, William J. (1964) *The Family* (New Jersey: Prentice-Hall).

Gornick, Vivian and Moran, Barbara K. (1971) *Woman in Sexist Society* (New York: Basic Books).

Granick, David (1960) *The Red Executive* (New York: Doubleday).

Grant, Nigel (1979) *Soviet Education* (Harmondsworth: Penguin).

Grunert-Bronnen, Barbara (1970) *Ich bin Bürger der DDR und lebe in der Bundesrepublik* (Munchen: Piper).

Haavio-Mannila Elina (1971) 'Satisfaction with Family, Work, Leisure, and Life among Men and Women', *Human Relations*, vol. 24, no. 6, pp. 585–601.

Hagstrom, Warren O. (1974) 'Competition in Science', *American Sociological Review*, vol. 39, no. 1 (Feb.) pp. 1–18.

Hall, Richard H. (1969) *Occupations and the Social Structure* (New Jersey: Prentice-Hall pp. 91–4.

Halsey, A. H., Floud, Jean, Anderson, C. Arnold (eds.) (1961) *Education, Economy, and Society* (New York: Free Press).

Hanhardt, Jr, Arthur M. (1968) *The German Democratic Republic* (Baltimore: Johns Hopkins University Press).

Hayghe, Howard (1975) 'Marital and Family Characteristics of the Labor Force', Special Labor Force Report 183, US Department of Labor, Bureau of Labor Statistics (March).

Heitlinger, Alena (1979) *Women and State Socialism, Sex Inequality in the Soviet Union and Czechoslovakia* (London: Macmillan)

Hoffman, L. and Nye, F. E. (eds.) (1974) *Working Mothers* (San Francisco: Jossey-Bass).

Hollander, Paul (1969) *American and Soviet Society* (New Jersey: Prentice-Hall).

Holmstrom, Lynda Lytle (1972) *The Two-Career Family* (Cambridge, Mass.: Schenkman).

Horner, Matina (1971) 'Fail: Bright Women', in Athena Theodore (ed.) *The Professional Woman* (Cambridge, Mass.: Schenkman).

Horney, Karen (1937) *The Neurotic Personality of our Time* (New York: Norton) .

Hughes, Everett C. (1956) 'The Making of a Physician – A General Statement of

Ideas and Problems', *Human Organization*, vol. 14 (Winter) pp. 21–5.

Inkeles, Alex and Geiger, Kent (1961) *Soviet Society* (Boston: Houghton Mifflin).

Inkeles, Alex (1966) 'Social Stratification and Mobility in the Soviet Union', in Bendix and Lipset (1966, pp. 516–26).

Jancar, Barbara Wolfe (1978) *Women Under Communism: A Cross-National Analysis of Women in Communist Societies* (Baltimore: Johns Hopkins University Press).

Juviler, Peter (1966) 'Soviet Families', *Survey* (July), pp. 51–61.

Kahn, R. L., Rosenthal, R. H. Wolfe, D. M., Quinn, R. P. and Snoek, J. D. (1964) *Organizational Stress: Studies in Role Conflict and Ambiguity* (New York: Wiley).

Kanter, Rosabeth Moss (1977) *Men and Women of the Corporation* (New York: Basic Books).

Kanter, Rosabeth Moss (1977) *Work and Family in the United States: A Critical Review and Agenda for Research and Policy* (New York: Russell Sage Foundation).

Kay, Emanuel (1974) 'Middle Management', in James O'Toole (ed.), *Work and the Quality of Life* (Cambridge, Mass.: MIT Press) pp. 106–29.

Koenig, René (1946) *Materialien zur Soziologie der Familie* (Bern: Francke).

Kollontai, Alexandra (1926/1975) *The Autobiography of a Sexually Emancipated Communist Woman* (New York: Schocken).

Krisch, Henry (1974) *German Politics Under Soviet Occupation* (New York: Columbia University Press).

Lane, David (1971) *The End of Inequality?* (Harmondsworth, Penguin).

Lapidus, Gail Warshofsky (1978) *Women in Soviet Society: Equality, Development and Social Change* (Berkeley: University of California Press).

Lein, Laura, *et al.* (1974) *Work and Family Life*, Final Report to the National Institute of Education (Cambridge, Mass.: Center for the Study of Public Policy).

Lipset, S. M. (1973) 'Stratification Research and Soviet Scholarship', in Murray Yanowich and Wesley A. Fisher (eds.) (New York: International Arts and Science Press), pp. 355–91.

Lortie, Dan C. (1966). 'Professional Socialization', in Vollmer and Mills (1966).

Ludz, Peter Christian (1970) *The German Democratic Republic from the Sixties to the Seventies* (Harvard University Center for International Affairs), Number 26.

Lynd, Robert S. and Lynd, Helen Merrell (1937) *Middletown, A Study in Modern American Culture* (New York: Harcourt, Brace and World).

Makarenko, Anton S. (1967) *The Collective Family*, translated by Robert Daglish (New York: Doubleday).

Malewski, A. (1974) 'Attitudes of the Employees from Warsaw Enterprises toward the Differentiation of Wages and the Social System in May 1958', Polish Sociological Association, *Polish Sociology* (Warsaw), pp. 176–90.

Mandel, William M. (1975) *Soviet Women* (New York: Anchor Press/Doubleday).

Marx, Karl (1963) *Early Writings*, ed. and trans. by T. B. Bottomore (New York: McGraw Hill).

Matthews, Mervyn (1972) *Class and Society in Soviet Russia* (New York: Walker).

Matthews, Mervyn (1978) *Privilege in the Soviet Union: A Study of Elite Life-Styles Under Communism* (London, Boston: Allen and Unwin).

McAuley, Alastair (1979) *Economic Welfare in the Soviet Union* (Hemel Hempstead: Allen and Unwin).

McClelland, David C. (1961) *The Achieving Society* (New York: Free Press).

Menschik, Jutta and Leopold, Evelyn (1974) *Gretchens Rote Schwestern* (Frankfurt am Main: Fischer)

Merton, Robert K. (1957) *Social Theory and Social Structure*, 2nd edn (New York: Free Press).

Merton, Robert K., Reader, George G. and Kendall, Patricia (eds.) (1957), *The Student-Physician* (Cambridge, Mass.: Harvard University Press).

Mills, C. Wright (1963) *Power, Politics and People* (New York: Ballantine Books).

Mizruchi, Ephraim, Harold (1964) 'Alienation and Anomie: Theoretical and Empirical Perspectives', in Horowitz, Irving Louis (ed.), *The New Sociology* (New York: Oxford University Press).

Montagu, Ashley (1962) *The Humanization of Man* (Cleveland and New York: World Publishing Company).

Morgan, Marabel (1976) *The Total Woman* (New York: Pocket Books).

Nosow, Sigmund and Form, William H. (1962) *Man, Work and Society* (New York: Basic Books).

Orzack, Louis H. (1959) 'Work as a "Central Life Interest" of Professionals', *Social Problems*, vol. VII, no. 2 (Fall) pp. 125–32.

Osipov, G. V. (ed.) (1966) *Industry and Labour in the U.S.S.R.* (London: Tavistock).

Paloma, Margaret, M. and Garland, T. Neal (1971), 'The Myth of the Egalitarian Family: Familial Roles and the Professionally Employed Wife', in Athena Theodore (ed.), *The Professional Woman* (Cambridge, Mass.: Schenkman).

Papanek, Hannah (1973) 'Men, Women, and Work: Reflections on the Two-Person Career', *American Journal of Sociology*, vol. 78, no. 4 (Jan.) pp. 852–72.

Parkin, Frank (1971) *Class Inequality and Political Order* (New York: Praeger).

Parsons, Talcott (1954) 'Age and Sex in the Social Structure of the United States', in *Essays in Sociological Theory* (Glencoe: Free Press).

Parsons, Talcott (1961) 'The School Class as a Social System: Some of its Functions in American Society' in Halsey, *et. al., op. cit.*

Rapoport, Rhona and Rapoport, Robert (1971). *Dual-Career Families* (Harmondsworth: Penguin).

Rapoport, Rhona and Rapoport, Robert (1976) *Dual-Career Families Re-examined* (New York: Harper and Row).

Reiss, Albert R., Jr. (1955) 'Occupational Mobility of Professional Workers', *American Sociological Review* (Dec.) pp. 693–700.

Rossi, Alice (1965) 'Barriers to the Career Choice of Engineering, Medicine, or Science Among American Women' (Cambridge: MIT Press).

Rothschild, Constantina Safilios (ed.) (1972) *Toward a Sociology of Women* (Lexington, Mass.: Xerox College Publishing).

Rueschemeyer, Dietrich (1973) *Lawyers and Their Society* (Cambridge, Mass.: Harvard University Press).

Rueschemeyer, Marilyn (1980) 'Social and Work Relations of Professional Women: an Academic Collective in the German Democratic Republic', *East Central Europe*, Fall.

Rutkevich, and Fillippov, F. R. (1973) 'Social Sources of Recruitment of the Intelligentsia', in *Social Stratification and Mobility in the U.S.S.R.*, Murray Yanowich and Wesley A. Fisher (eds.) (New York: International Arts and Science Press), pp. 241–74.

Sacks, Michael Paul (1976) *Women's Work in Soviet Russia; Continuity in the Midst of Change* (New York: Praeger).

Sarapata, Adam (1974) 'Iustum Pretium', *Polish Sociological Association*, Polish Sociology (Warsaw) pp. 160–175.

Scott, Hilda (1974) *Does Socialism Liberate Women?* (Boston: Beacon Press).

Scott, Richard W. (1966) 'Professionals in Bureaucracies–Areas of Conflict', in Vollmer (1966, pp. 265–75).

Seeley, J., Sim, R., and Looseley, E. (1956) *Crestwood Heights* (New York: Basic Books).

Sève, Lucien (1975) *Marxism and the Theory of Human Personality* (London: Lawrence and Wishart).

Silverman, Charles E. (1970) *Crisis in the Classroom* (New York: Random House).

Smith, Hedrick (1976) *The Russians* (New York: Quadrangle, New York Times Book Co.) pp. 147–50.

Social Problems (1961) vol. 9, no. 1, an issue devoted to Leisure.

Sokolowska, Magdalena (1965) 'Some Reflections on the Different Attitudes of Men and Women Towards Work', *International Labor Review* (July).

Stein, Maurice (1960) *The Eclipse of Community* (Princeton: Princeton University Press).

Sugarman, Barry (1973) *The School and Moral Development* (London: Croom Helm).

Theodore, Athena (ed.) (1971) *The Professional Woman* (Cambridge, Mass.: Schenkman).

Veroff, Joseph and Feld, Sheila (1970) *Marriage and Work in America* (New York: Van Nostrand-Reinhold).

Vollmer, Howard M. and Mills. Donald L. (eds) (1966) *Professionalization* (New Jersey: Prentice-Hall).

Warner, W. Lloyd and Abegglen, James C. (1963) *Big Business Leaders in America* (New Jersey: Atheneum).

Warner, W. Lloyd and Martin, Norman H. (1959) *Industrial Man, Businessmen and Business Organizations* (New York: Harper).

Weiss, Robert S. (1969) 'The Fund of Sociability', in *Trans-action* (July/August), pp. 36–43.

Weiss, Robert S., Harwood Edwin and Riesman, David (1961) 'Work and Automation: Problems and Prospects', in Merton, Robert K. and Nisbet, Robert (eds.), *Contemporary Social Problems* (New York: Harcourt, Brace and World).

White, Stephen (1979) *Political Culture and Soviet Politics*, (London: Macmillan, and New York: St Martins).

Whyte, William H. (1956) *The Organization Man* (New York: Doubleday).

Wilenski, Harold (1963) 'The Uneven Distribution of Leisure: the Impact of Economic Growth on "Free-Time"', in Erwin O. Smigel, *Work and Leisure* (New Haven, Conn.: College and University Press).

Yanowich, Murray and Fisher, Wesley A. (eds.) (1973) *Social Stratification and Mobility in the U.S.S.R.* (New York: International Arts and Science Press).

Young, Michael and Peter Willmott (1973) *The Symmetrical Family* (London: Routledge and Kegan Paul).

Index

Abegglen, J., 8
Absorption in work, *see* Work, absorption in
Achievement orientation, 8, 34, 37–9, 40, 46, 79, 119–20, 122, 124
Agyris, C., 180n
Alcoholism, 9, 152
Alienation, 2–3, 9, 14, 21, 164, 170–1, 176–7, 183n
Ambition, 2, 4, 5, 13; of American women for their husbands, 47, 53–4, 170; causes of, 6, 20, 37, 62; in dual-career families, 87–8, 172; and early career experiences, 6, 14, 28–9, 41–2, 50–1; effects of lack of ambition, 35; effects on personal life in US, 8–10; effects on personality, 9; and family background, 35, 37, 72–8; in GDR and USSR, 13, 19–21; increase of, among professional women, 84; limitations of, 7, 13; of parents for their children, 37, 73, 78; in school, 6, 20, 37; and self-employed professionals, 35; among single- and dual-career American males, 33–4, 47, 173; of single-career wives, 48
Anderson, B., 12, 181n
Atkinson, D., 12
Attitudes: developed in early stages of career, 6, 28–9, 33, 85, 130–1, 138–9
Authority: tensions with, 9, 27–9, 33, 86; at work, 17, 27–8, 33, 130, 138–9
Autonomy: of professionals, 2, 6, 177

Background, social: and ambition, 35, 72–8; of East European professionals, 116–19; of men in single-

career families, 35–7; of respondents in dual-career families, 72–8; of women in single-career families, 25–6; *see also* Social mobility
Bailyn, L., 183n
Bartolmé, F., 8–9
Becker, H., 180n
Blau, P., 19
Blauner, R., 2, 183n
Blue-collar work: and nature of professional work, 2
Bronfenbrenner, U., 122–4, 182n
Brown, A., 20, 149
Bureaucracy: professionals in, 7–8, 13, 30, 32, 86, 129

Capitalism: competitive behaviour in, 8–9, 62, 177–8; contrasts and similarities with socialist societies, 5, 10–13, 112, 122–3, 157, 170, 173–9; professionals in, 2–10, 23–111; school in, 38–41, 78–81
Caplow, T., 180n, 182n
Careers: choice of, 4, 17, 20, 35, 37, 124–5, 127; early stages of, 4, 14, 28–9, 41–2, 50–1, 130, 138–9; hopes of single-career wives during later stages of, 42; *see also* Social mobility, Social relationships
Carper, J., 180n
Chafe, W., 8, 180–1n
Child-care: in American dual-career families, 83–99, 108; in GDR and USSR, 13, 133–7, 175; *see also* Cribbes
Children: attitudes toward, 1–2, 8–9, 54, 94–5, 109, 120–1, 136–7; and traditional sex roles, 92, 196–8; in US dual-career families, 74, 88–90